COMMODITIES BY FREIGHT CAR

Jeff Wilson

Kalmbach
Media

On the cover (clockwise from top left): This Chicago, Burlington & Quincy AAR three-bay, 70-ton hopper was built in 1951, rebuilt in 1962, and photographed in 1963. *John Ingles; J. David Ingles collection.* The Pennsylvania Railroad built its G41A coil steel cars in the late 1960s; this one still serves Conrail in 1984. *J. David Ingles.* A former Rock Island 2,600-cf Airslide car is in flour service in 1982; it was built in 1968. *J. David Ingles collection.* Brach's leased a fleet of Airslide covered hoppers, including this 4,180-cf car, to carry sugar. It's shown in 1974. *J. David Ingles.* This 10,800-gallon, ICC 105A 500W pressure tank car is carrying liquid chlorine for owner Hooker Chemicals in 1981. *J. David Ingles.* This Grand Trunk Western 73-foot center-beam lumber car was built by Gunderson and photographed around 2000. *Jeff Wilson.* A forklift loads auto-parts racks into a Southern Pacific 86-foot high-cube boxcar built by Pacific Car & Foundry. *Southern Pacific.*

Back cover (clockwise from top left): Fruit Growers Express pioneered development of mechanical reefers for frozen-food service; this car was built in 1956 and photographed in 1961. *John Ingles; J. David Ingles collection.* General American's Pressure Slide tank-style covered hoppers were designed for cement. This Chicago, Burlington & Quincy car was built in 1967 and photographed in 1978. *R.J. Wilhelm; J. David Ingles collection.* A worker places a flour-loading pipe in position over a covered-hopper hatch at a Cargill mill in the 1980s. *CSX*

On the facing page: The United States Railroad Administration two-bay, 50-ton hopper was the first common coal car design built in large numbers. This Colorado & Southern (Chicago, Burlington & Quincy subsidiary) car, built in 1919, is shown in 1959. *J. David Ingles*

Acknowledgements:
Thanks to *Classic Trains* magazine editor Brian Schmidt, who provided the idea for this project. Further inspiration came from poring through the freight-car slide collection of the late J. David Ingles, with most of the images in the collection taken by Dave or his father, John Ingles. I thank others who provided photographs for this book, including Cody Grivno, Jim Hediger, James Kinkaid, Keith Kohlmann, and Jeff Lemke. I'm also thankful for all of the photographers—especially for those shooting in the steam and early diesel eras—whose photos reside at the David P. Morgan Library at Kalmbach Media. Without all of their contributions, this book would not have been possible.

Kalmbach Media
21027 Crossroads Circle
Waukesha, Wisconsin 53186
www.KalmbachHobbyStore.com

Published in 2023
27 26 25 24 23   1 2 3 4 5

Manufactured in China

ISBN: 978-162700-941-6
EISBN: 978-162700-942-3

Editor: Steven Otte
Book Design: Lisa Bergmann

Library of Congress Control Number: 2022948400

Contents

Introduction 4

Chapter 1
Grain 6

Chapter 2
Chlorine 20

Chapter 3
Lumber 26

Chapter 4
Cement.. 36

Chapter 5
Coil steel.. 46

Chapter 6
Liquified petroleum gas (propane and butane) ...56

Chapter 7
Flour and sugar... 64

Chapter 8
Coal.. 72

Chapter 9
Auto parts 84

Chapter 10
Frozen foods 94

Chapter 11
Wood chips 102

Bibliography 111

Introduction

Freight cars have become highly specialized, a continuing evolution that started with coal hopper cars in the 1800s and continued through cement covered hoppers in the 1930s, piggyback flats in the 1950s, coil-steel cars and grain covered hoppers in the 1960s, and center-beam flatcars for lumber in the 1980s. This book is a guide to the freight cars that have been historically used to carry various products—not necessarily the most common ones, but those that provide interesting loads or models or offer opportunities for interesting operations.

You don't have to model the industries involved to model the cars carrying various products. Simply having a knowledge of what the different types of cars are carrying will make the models more interesting and make your operations more realistic. If you do model an industry, vendor, or business served by these cars, knowing more about the cars—their evolution, restrictions, and how commodities are loaded and secured—will make your industries more realistic.

Look for opportunities to detail cars with loads, even for cars that are normally closed. Examples include placing a boxcar with open doors at the end of a spur with its load visible (perhaps bagged flour or cement, or a boxcar with grain doors installed, appearing ready for loading at an elevator), or an Airslide covered hopper or tank car with piping connected to simulate active loading or unloading. Closed cars can have loads indicated by how they're weathered and by lettering (such as commodity stenciling, hazmat placards, and "RETURN TO …" lettering).

Car evolution

Railroads historically have been loath to adopt specialty freight cars. To railroads through most of the steam era, the beauty of plain boxcars, gondolas, and flatcars was that they could carry just about anything. When a car was unloaded, it was immediately ready for another load. Railroads did not want to invest in single-commodity cars, as they would only be loaded at most half of the time, limiting their ability to generate revenue. This is why many such cars were slow to catch on, were operated in small numbers, or became largely privately owned—at least until railroads figured they would pay off financially with a high enough volume of traffic. Tank and refrigerator cars are prime examples.

Car identification

There have been a tremendous number of prototype car designs built through the years. The information in each

This Trailer Train bulkhead flat was built in 1975. It's carrying a load of wrapped, bundled lumber in May 1976. Many freight cars have evolved significantly to carry specific products or commodities; others, like this car, can carry a variety of goods.
J. David Ingles

chapter is designed to help identify the general type of cars used, and in many cases specific manufacturers (or AAR car types) or models. However, there simply isn't enough space to go into great detail on all the spotting features and variations that many cars have gone through during their production. Entire books have been written about single car types and models. If you're interested, do a search on the internet; also, the bibliography on page 111 lists some specific articles and books that may help you.

Modeling

We're lucky to live in a period where so many models have been produced through the years that you can often track down models of specific prototypes and variations. Along with plastic models, check the offerings from resin kit manufacturers (Funaro & Camerlengo, Resin Car Works, Smoky Mountain Model Works, Speedwitch Media, Sunshine Models, Westerfield, Yarmouth Model Works, and others). Even though many resin models are limited-edition kits, older ones can often be tracked down online. The same is true for limited-edition or out-of-production plastic kits: If it has been made, you can probably find it through eBay or other online sources.

Another option is 3-D printing. A number of vendors offer 3-D printed models through Shapeways.com, and the number of available models in this medium is growing.

Resources

The Official Railway Equipment Register (ORER) is an indispensable guide for car rosters and details. I highly recommend tracking down an issue that matches the era you're modeling. Published quarterly, the ORER is the official publication listing all cars in service for a given time, and copies can be found from many vendors. Westerfield offers digital versions of many issues on DVD.

Each chapter includes references to additional resources, as does the bibliography. Thousands of books have been published about freight cars—do an internet search to see what's out there—and modeling magazines have published countless articles including details on spotting features, variations, histories, and rosters of many car types, including articles on how to model them. Many generous modelers and photographers have also shared their work online.

I hope this book helps increase your knowledge about cars and what they carry. Keep digging into the subjects that interest you the most (and are most relevant to your layout), and your models, industries, and operations will become more realistic.

Car capacity and clearances

A common theme through the evolution of various freight car types has been a steady increase in size and weight capacity from the steam era through today. Cars are often known by their nominal capacity in tons (50-, 70-, 100-, or 110-ton cars), but that's just a rough estimate. The key number is the car's gross rail load (GRL), which is the total weight on rails allowed for the car. It's calculated by adding a car's light weight and load limit (found in the data on the left side of each car).

The Association of American Railroads (AAR) sets standards for GRL limits for unrestricted interchange (with additional higher limits for restricted interchange); these limits have risen over the years as railroads have improved bridges and track structure. Into the early 1960s, this meant 50-ton cars (169,000 pounds, or 169K) for unrestricted interchange, although most routes allowed 70-ton (210K) cars and many allowed 100-ton (251K).

In 1963 the limits for each weight class were increased: to 177K GRL for 50-ton cars, 220K for 70-ton, and 263K for 100-ton. This marked the start of the 100-ton-car era, as most major routes allowed the cars. Many branch lines remained restricted to 50- or 70-ton cars; in fact, the move to 100-ton cars was what doomed many branch lines.

Railroads had begun using 110-ton cars (286K GRL) on some routes by the early 1990s, and the AAR officially approved the weight class for interchange in 1995.

Physical car size is another set of specifications. The AAR publishes Plate designations for size, each having a diagram with maximum dimensions at various car heights, coupled with length specifications. Plate B cars (first adopted in 1948) are unrestricted. Plate C (1963) cars are allowed on most routes. Taller cars are more restricted on routes, and fall under Plate E, F, H, J, and K diagrams.

CHAPTER ONE

Grain

Covered hoppers took over most grain traffic by the early 1970s. The Pullman-Standard 4,427-cf car was one of the most popular early grain cars. This is a late version, known as a "high side" car, with 13 side posts. It was built in 1966 and leased to Louis-Dreyfus (it carries the TLDX reporting marks of Pullman Leasing). The large LDC logo is bolted to the side posts. *J. David Ingles*

Railroads have carried grain—and lots of it—since the 1800s. Most grain traffic is corn (54 percent of carloads), wheat (19 percent), and soybeans (15 percent), but railroads also haul significant amounts of sorghum (milo), rye, barley, oats, and rice. Grain accounts for about a million carloads annually, about 7 percent of total rail traffic.

This Chicago Great Western boxcar carries a load of corn—visible behind the wood grain doors—in this early 1970s view. The side door has been opened as it's about to head into the elevator for unloading. *Richard Cecil*

Each type of grain has many varieties, all destined for different uses. Grains are the raw materials for many food and consumer products, and railroads move grain from elevators in growing areas to storage elevators, food processors, and flour and feed mills across the country, and to export elevators on the coasts.

Grain traffic has historically been heavily seasonal, with traffic peaking as various crops are harvested, starting with the South in late summer to the huge wheat fields of the northern U.S. and western Canada in late fall. This has been mitigated somewhat since the 1970s, as local elevators and farms all have increased storage capabilities and can hold grain as needed based on prices and demand. Although grain traffic still generally peaks in late fall, loaded grain cars move year round.

From the steam era well into the

Paper grain doors, reinforced with metal straps, became more common by the 1970s; this one is from Signode, the major supplier. They were cut open at the receiving elevator. *Signode Corp.*

To load a boxcar, the flexible loading spout ("slinger") from the elevator is clamped to the top grain door. The worker then directs the spout to distribute the grain into the car. *Arthur Rothstein, Library of Congress*

1960s, the standard means of carrying grain was the 40-foot, 50-ton boxcar. As is noted throughout this book, railroads have always been reluctant to invest in single-commodity cars, and grain traffic was no exception. Even though the covered hopper had been around since the 1930s, it wasn't until the mid-1960s that covered hoppers began carrying grain in significant amounts, and boxcars still hauled plenty of grain through the 1970s.

Grain boxcars

Although grain was sometimes shipped in bags into the early 1900s, most of it was simply carried in boxcars in bulk. An exception was high-value grain, especially seeds, which could be easily contaminated.

To carry bulk grain, boxcars needed to be sealed to keep grain from escaping. Floors and walls needed to be solid, with no cracks or holes. The big challenge was temporarily covering the side door openings. Around 1900, several attempts were made to design hinged or gated doors that would stay with the car and fold out of the way, but to no avail.

The usual solution was nailing wood planks horizontally across the opening from inside. This worked, but boards were inconsistent in size and quality, and there was a lot of waste as boards were often broken and discarded, just like dunnage for other cars.

By the mid-1930s, the solution became the reusable grain door. Each grain door was made from multiple boards, with each door measuring 7 feet long and either 10" or 20" wide. Multiple doors were nailed inside the car door openings to the needed height; the process was known as "coopering." Grain doors were stenciled with the owning railroad's initials, and were collected at grain terminals and milling districts (by the Western Weighing and Inspection Bureau) and

By the late 1950s, many large elevators and grain terminals used car dumpers that could pivot and turn boxcars to unload grain. This one also has an arm that reaches into the car to scoop out the remaining grain. *Glidden Co.*

The Chicago, Burlington & Quincy built this 50-foot, 70-ton, double-plug-door exterior-post boxcar at its Havelock Shops in 1964. The right-hand door has two small doors at top (painted gray); one is used for filling the car with grain, the other for inspection. *John Ingles; J. David Ingles collection*

Southern's aluminum-body Big John cars, built by Magor, were the first true grain-service covered hoppers. This one, built in 1962, has round roof hatches; later versions had trough-style hatches. *John Ingles; J. David Ingles collection*

returned to the owning railroads.

Disposable paper grain doors (reinforced with steel straps) began appearing in large numbers by the 1960s. These were installed in the same manner, but were torn away to unload the car, with the scrap disposed of.

Boxcars were loaded at elevators by guiding a flexible loading spout into the car above the grain doors. The spout was directed to each end and then the middle of the car until the load was at the desired height. Cars could also be loaded by portable augers or conveyors. Many cars included lines painted on the inside walls to indicate proper levels for each type of grain (lower for corn, higher for wheat).

Unloading boxcars was labor- and time-intensive. The grain doors would be knocked away (wood) or cut (paper) and the grain allowed to pour into grated openings next to the tracks. The remaining grain would be pushed and shoveled out of the car, sometimes with power-assisted shovels. By the 1950s, many large grain terminals were equipped with car dumpers that would clamp a boxcar in place and rotate it in multiple directions over a pit to empty the grain.

To eliminate the need for separate grain doors, several railroads in the 1960s equipped fleets of boxcars (new or rebuilt) with plug doors that had pairs of small swinging doors at top. This allowed the loading chute to go into one opening and the other to be used for inspection. Union Pacific (4,200 cars); Chicago, Burlington & Quincy (800); Atchison, Topeka & Santa Fe (450); and Soo Line (200) all operated cars of various designs.

Boxcars could be found in large numbers in grain service through the early 1970s, but by the end of that decade, covered hoppers had taken over most grain traffic. The 40-foot boxcar was disappearing rapidly, and the final jobs for many of them before scrapping was carrying grain from soon-to-be-

Pullman-Standard introduced its 4,000-cf covered hopper in 1962. Chicago, Burlington & Quincy no. 85512 was built in 1963 with round roof hatches. It's still hauling grain for Burlington Northern in this 1983 view. *Jeff Wilson collection*

This is an early ("low-side") version of the PS 4,427-cf car, built in April 1964 and leased to Bunge. It has a trough-style hatch with a single long cover; this design was changed shortly to have four overlapping hatches over a single long opening. *Pullman-Standard*

abandoned branch lines that couldn't handle 100-ton cars.

Grain covered hoppers

Even though covered hoppers had successfully been carrying cement and other products since the 1930s, very little grain was carried in covered hoppers until the 1960s. The existing larger three-bay cars were mainly used for potash, carbon black, phosphate, fertilizer, and other products, not grain.

The main reason grain remained in boxcars was rates: railroads weren't allowed to discount rates for hauling grain in covered hoppers, even through they were more efficient, could carry twice as much grain, and were easier to load and unload.

The first "jumbo" (100-ton) covered hoppers designed specifically for grain were the Southern's 4,713-cubic-foot (cf) aluminum cars first built in 1960 by Magor, nicknamed "Big John" cars. The railroad eventually acquired 775 similar cars through 1965. The railroad planned to give shippers discounted rates (compared to boxcars) for using multiple Big John cars. However, in 1961 the ICC stopped the railroad from applying the new rates. This was significant, because without the rates, there was no incentive for shippers to use the new cars and no incentive for railroads to invest in the new equipment.

It took multiple appeals and eventually a U.S. Supreme Court ruling (in 1963) before the Southern was allowed to implement its rates. The ruling gave the push to railroads to acquire fleets of covered hoppers dedicated to grain service.

Several details differentiated grain cars from covered hoppers carrying other products. First was size: the low-density weight of most grains allowed larger cars, and the adoption of the 100-ton car (263K GRL) in 1963 meant grain cars could be bigger than earlier cars: 4,000 cf and larger. Grain cars are often referred to simply by their cubic-foot capacities.

Earlier cars were built with individual loading hatches, but the car-length "trough" hatch soon became standard for grain cars. Grain didn't

This Pullman-Standard 4,750-cf covered hopper, built in 1974, is owned by North American Car Corp., which in turn leased it to the Farmers Co-op Elevator Co. of Albert City, Iowa. Pink was a popular color for cars leased by elevators. *R.J. Wilhelm; J. David Ingles collection*

Covered hopper ownership

Railroads owned the bulk of grain-service covered hoppers through the 1970s, but grain companies (including ADM, Bunge, Cargill, Louis-Dreyfus, Peavey, and others) began buying or leasing them (from the leasing divisions of the car builders) in the 1960s to ensure a consistent supply of cars. Private ownership increased through the 1980s and later, and today a majority of grain cars are privately owned. Early cars often had separate signboards for their owners/lessees attached to the car, spanning two or more vertical posts.

Even as the number of grain covered hoppers increased, some elevators had problems getting enough cars to handle their traffic. A solution was for elevators to lease cars, thus guaranteeing they'd get their cars back for reloading. These often had bright color schemes with the elevator name in large lettering. Many kept their original schemes even after the leases expired and they were sold to other owners.

The PS 4740 has 16 evenly spaced side posts. This Northern Pacific version was built in 1969; it's shown in service on Burlington Northern around 1980. *J. David Ingles collection*

Pullman-Standard's 4,750-cf car was the most popular early grain car. It can be identified by its 18 tubular side posts. This one, built in 1974, is leased to The Andersons. *Pullman-Standard*

Late 4750s from PS have an angled top strip above the middle 12 side posts. This former Peavey car, built in 1979, has been restenciled for new owners twice by the time of this 2003 photo, when it was owned by short line Minnesota Prairie Line. *Jeff Wilson*

The PS 4,475-cf car was comparatively rare; it can be spotted by its 13 evenly spaced posts. This Cargill leased car was built in July 1966.

John Ingles; J. David Ingles collection

require the tight seal that cement and food products required, and the long opening made loading much easier. Some early cars had single trough-length hatch covers; this was soon changed to four overlapping hatches over a single long opening.

Most grain cars have three gravity-style outlet bays, allowing fast dumping into between-the-rails catch bins. Cars with pneumatic outlets—marked by a horizontal pipe across the bottom of a V-shaped bay—are more common in plastic pellet, chemical, or food-product service.

Grain cars would be built in two major styles: with vertical side walls and exterior vertical posts (braces), or with smooth, curved side walls, with the curves providing structural strength in the manner of a tank. In spotting/ identifying variations of grain cars, look at the overall size (height and length); number, style, and pattern of vertical posts; style of roof hatches; and the end platform style and bracing pattern.

Pullman-Standard and ACF grain cars

The 1960s and 1970s were dominated by grain cars from two manufacturers: Pullman-Standard (PS) and ACF Industries (formerly American Car & Foundry). Each offered 100-ton cars in various sizes and dimensions to match Plate B and Plate C clearances.

In 1962, PS introduced its three-bay, 4,000-cf grain car. The new design looked much like the company's earlier covered hoppers, but taller, and was designated PS-2CD, with the "CD" standing for "center discharge." This referred to a single outlet gate centered under each bay. The grain car car was distinctive, with tall sides and a 4-3-4 vertical post pattern on each side.

A larger 4,427-cf version introduced by PS in 1964 proved to be one of the most popular grain cars of the decade, with more than 23,000 built through 1971. Early versions were known as "low-side" cars, as the sides extended down to just above the truck sideframes; cars from 1966 onward were "high-side" cars, with 13 evenly spaced vertical posts and the bottoms

Boxcar and covered hopper fleets

Although grain covered hoppers increased greatly in number through the 1960s, it wasn't until 1972 that they outnumbered boxcars in grain service. In that year, covered hoppers carried 54 percent of grain carloads and 63 percent of total grain tonnage. By 1979, there were 177,223 covered hoppers in grain service and just 63,530 boxcars; grain boxcars were virtually gone just two years later, although they survived on some western Canadian branch lines through the 1980s.

The first Center Flow cars from ACF were nearly cylindrical. This three-bay, 3,700-cf Union Pacific car, built in 1964, has three separate long hatches. *Union Pacific*

of the sides higher, leaving more of the outlet bays exposed.

A slightly larger car, the 4,740-cf PS-2CD, was offered from 1966 to 1971, with more than 10,000 built. This design can be spotted by its 16 evenly spaced side posts.

The most-popular PS grain car was the 4,750-cf version, with about 56,000 built from 1972 until PS ceased operations in 1981. The car retained the same basic appearance as earlier cars, but with 18 side posts. Variations include notches at the bottom of each side post (starting in 1973), the addition of a horizontal angled top strip atop the middle 12 side posts (1979), and a visible hole in the center sill between each outlet bay (1979).

Pullman-Standard built PS-2CDs in other sizes as well, with larger versions used for plastic pellets, malted barley, and other lightweight products. Two rare versions that sometimes carried grain are the 4,475-cf car (13 side posts, deeper/lower sides than the 4,427) and the 4,785-cf car, which looked like the 4,750 but with deeper sides (the side sill isn't readily visible).

ACF Industries entered the grain

Great Northern no. 171002 is an example of an early six-bay, 3,960-cf Center Flow car. Built in December 1963, it has round hatches above each compartment/bay. *John Ingles; J. David Ingles collection*

ACF's most-popular early grain car was the 4,650-cf Center Flow. This former Great Northern (now Burlington Northern) car is an early version, with the single horizontal stiffener running along the top of the side. *Jeff Wilson collection*

In 1973, Illinois Central bought 100 fiberglass covers from Proform and installed them on coal hoppers to help cover the fall grain rush. Each weighed 2,800 pounds and cost $2,650. *Illinois Central Gulf*

Several Rock Island (former Missouri-Kansas-Texas) stock cars are ready for grain loading in Topeka, Kan., in 1971. Plywood interior sheathing has been applied to hold the grain. *J. David Ingles collection*

Converted open hoppers and stock cars

Through the 1970s, the fall grain rush created a high demand for grain cars, a problem exacerbated as the number of 40-foot boxcars was declining rapidly by the late 1960s. One solution several railroads employed was adding covers to open hoppers to carry grain. Proform was one company that offered fiberglass covers; the photo at left shows one being installed on an Illinois Central Gulf coal hopper. Other railroads used home-built covers or tarps, or sometimes ran the cars open. These options obviously weren't ideal and were generally short-term to alleviate severe car shortages.

Stock cars were another solution in the late 1960s and early 1970s. The drop in livestock traffic in the early 1960s meant many railroads in Plains states had lots of stock cars sitting idle or bound for scrap. The interiors were lined with plywood to use them for grain. Since they were typically smaller than boxcars, a common arrangement was to assign them to elevators in pairs.

The second-most-popular 100-ton Center Flow grain car was the 4,600-cf version, which was longer but not as tall as the 4650. This BNSF car is a later version, with the distinctive corrugated horizontal piece along the side/roof joint. *Jeff Wilson*

FMC's grain cars are easy to spot by the horizontal groove running down the center of each side. This Burlington Northern car is a 4,700-cf version, identified by its 16 evenly spaced side posts. *Jeff Wilson*

car field with a radical new design: the Center Flow car. The first, built in 1961, was nearly cylindrical—the company called it an "inverted pear-shape" cross section. The curved sides provided tank-like strength, eliminating the need for side posts, and side sills eliminated the need for a center sill, making it very efficient to load and unload. The first had individual roof hatches and either 3,510-cf (three-bay) or 3,960-cf (six-bay) bodies; a 3,700-cf three-bay version with trough hatches soon appeared.

To increase capacity, ACF soon revised the design. The cross-section was flattened, creating what ACF termed the "teardrop" design. The side

walls became noticeably flatter, but still curved. The first grain version of this car, introduced in 1964, was the popular 4,650-cf, three-bay, trough-hatch version. Almost 16,000 would be built through 1982.

A similar version was introduced in 1965, the 4,600-cf three-bay car. It was two feet longer and 5 inches shorter in height than the 4,650, built for the more-restrictive Plate B clearance preferred by some buyers. About 15,000 were built through 1981. Two other versions were built in smaller quantities: the 4,460, which is the same length as the 4,650 but not as tall; and the 4,700, which looks like the 4,600 but has shallower end sheets.

The Center Flow cars had one distinctive modification during production: Early cars have a single horizontal stiffener located near the top of each side. In August 1970 this changed, with later cars having multiple horizontal corrugations along the seam between the top of the side and edge of the roof.

Other 100-ton grain cars
FMC built three covered hoppers popular for grain. At first glance they resemble PS cars, but the FMC cars have a distinctive horizontal groove down the middle of each side. The 4,700-cf version has 16 side posts; the 4,692-cf car has a 5/4/5 post pattern;

Canadian railroads favored cylindrical covered hoppers for grain and other products. This is a four-bay 3,400-cf car with round roof hatches built in 1965 for Canadian Pacific. *John Ingles; J. David Ingles collection*

This Alberta Heritage Fund covered hopper is assigned to Canadian National. The 4,550-cf car was built in 1981 and is rolling through Waukesha, Wis., in 2003. *J. David Ingles*

The Trinity 5,161-cf covered hopper is the most-common modern (110-ton) car in grain service. Note the distinctive lip where the rounded roof overhangs the side. This one is on BNSF in 2006. *Jeff Wilson*

and the 4,526-cf car has a 4/3/4 post pattern.

Thrall offered a 100-ton, 4,750-cf grain car that initially had posts in a 6-4-6 pattern. By the 1970s, this had changed to 16 vertical side posts, resembling a PS car. The Thrall car differed in that the end posts on each side were U channels, and the side sills stepped down at the end platforms.

Trinity began building a 4,750-cf covered hopper in the late 1970s. It had 18 side posts, an arched roof with raised middle section (along the trough), and a different design at the bolsters compared to PS cars. Trinity acquired the PS designs in 1984, and its cars after that strongly resembled the final PS designs.

Evans built two common grain designs: a 4,750-cf car built from kits supplied by (and thus nearly identical to) PS, and a 4,780-cf car that has a 5/4/5 post pattern. North American also built 4,750-cf cars from PS kits.

Several minor builders also built covered hoppers, including Ingalls Shipbuilding (18 side posts, rounded roof, and car-length eaves that wrap from the roof around the tops of the side posts) and Richmond Tank Car (car-length eaves, 18 or 19 side posts, and arched roofs).

Canadian railroads relied on cylindrical cars similar to the early Center Flow design. These cars were built by the thousands by multiple builders from 1965 to 1985. Cars grew in size, with early 3,400- to 3,850-cf cars 50 or 52 feet long with four bays. These were owned by Canadian National and Canadian Pacific and hauled potash as well as grain. After 1973, most cars were 4,100- to 4,550-cf four-bay cars, 59 feet long. Many were operated by the Canadian Wheat Board, Saskatchewan Grain Car Corp., and the province of Alberta, and were assigned to either CN or CP (by having an N or P in the reporting marks).

Most of these 100-ton cars had long lifespans, typically close to 40 years (the mandatory retirement age without rebuilding). Many were sold to secondary owners or transferred after their original leases expired (often to short lines and regional railroads); these were sometimes completely repainted but usually simply had their reporting marks painted out and new ones stenciled in place.

Modern covered hoppers

When the 110-ton car (286K GRL) became standard in 1995, larger grain cars quickly appeared. Most of these

The ARI 5,200-cf Center Flow grain car has the same design at the roof/side joint as earlier ACF Center Flow 100-ton cars. This Union Pacific car, built in 2005, is shown in 2006. *Jeff Wilson*

This 5,155-cf covered hopper was built by NSC. Note the wide horizontal panel where the side meets the roof, and the step-down where the side meets the end above the bolster. *Jeff Wilson*

new grain cars resemble ACF's Center Flow, as ACF's original patents began expiring. Manufacturers copied the curved-side design, but with distinctive variations. In spotting these cars, look for the size (cubic capacity, length, and height), style of roof (including the joint with the top of the side), side sill (straight through end platforms or stepped), number of side panels (separated by vertical weld seams), style of running boards (and number of support brackets) and roof hatches,

and the design of the ends (shape, angle, and height of the cutout and the arrangement of braces and ladders).

The most popular of the new cars has been Trinity's 5,161-cf car, with more than 27,000 built through 2020. This car has a roof that slightly overhangs the side and 10 or 12 side panels. The shape of the ends has changed over the years, and some older 5161s have received reinforcing panels at the end of each side. Trinity also builds a 5,204-cf car, with nine

side panels, and has also built some exterior-post 5,127- and 5,160-cf cars—a rare design in the 110-ton car era.

The Center Flow is still built by American Railcar Industries (ARI), which is now the carbuilding division of ACF. The 5,200-cf car is common for grain, and can be spotted by its 11 side panels, the step down from side sill to end platform, and the ACF-style corrugations along the roof/side seam.

Greenbrier built this 5,200-cf covered hopper for BNSF in August 2020. Greenbrier cars have a distinctive groove in the top horizontal member along the side, and the end slope sheets start lower than the Trinity 5161 at left. *Cody Grivno*

FreightCar America's 5,200-cf grain car is quite similar to the Greenbrier car (top), but has different end bracing and end cutout patterns (it's coupled to a Greenbrier car at right and a Trinity car at left). *Cody Grivno*

National Steel Car has built 5,116-, 5,146-, and 5,155-cf cars. Compared to the Trinity cars, these have a wider horizontal seam at the tops of the sides, different end angle design, and a steep step down at the sides above the bolsters.

Greenbrier (Gunderson until the 1990s) has built 5,200-, 5,250-cf, and 5,188-cf grain cars. These have a horizontal notch in the seam between the sides and the distinctly curved roof. The 5,188 has horizontal corrugations in the center side panels.

FreightCar America makes a 5,200-cf car that's quite similar to the Greenbrier design, but with different bracing on the car ends, wider running-board supports on the roof, and a different shape on the angled end cutout on each side.

Thrall built a 5,150-cf similar to the ARI car, but with a thicker, heavier side sill that continues straight through the end platforms. Thrall was acquired by Trinity in 2001.

Further information

For a complete description of the grain industry, along with details about elevators, grain cars, train operations, and loading/unloading procedures, see Jeff Wilson's *The Model Railroader's Guide to Grain* (Kalmbach, 2015). *Grain Cars 1995/1996*, by David G. Casdorph (Society of Freight Car Historians, 1995) is an excellent overview of first-generation grain covered hoppers.

CHAPTER TWO

Chlorine

Chlorine-service tank cars are insulated pressure cars. This Union Tank Line car, leased to Hooker Chemicals, was built in 1957 and is shown in May 1959. It's a 10,500-gallon car with a center sill and an ICC 105A 300W specification. It has "FOR CHLORINE ONLY" stenciled on the right side. It was built by Union (Graver). *John Ingles; J. David Ingles collection*

Chlorine is among the most hazardous materials transported by rail, but it's a vital commodity as an ingredient in cleaning and disinfectant products, as a bleaching agent, in paper production, in water purification, and in a variety of industrial processes. Getting chlorine from manufacturing plants to industrial users has been done via tank car since the 1920s.

The most common method of producing chlorine is with electrolysis in a brine (sodium chloride, or salt) solution. To do this on a large scale requires a great deal of electricity, and thus chlorine is generally produced at large chemical plants.

Chlorine is a gas at room temperature, but liquifies readily under pressure—around 100 psi at 70 degrees F—making it more efficient to store and transport. This means specifications for chlorine are very similar to that of LPG (see Chapter 6), but chlorine is much denser; a gallon of chlorine weighs 10 pounds, more than double the 4.6 pounds of LPG. Chlorine is an inhalation hazard and reacts with many materials. This means all pressure vessels, connection points, valves, and seals must be as fail-safe as possible.

Tank cars carrying chlorine are distinctive, and most modelers of the 1930s to the present will be able to find logical reasons to include a car or two in their trains.

Early chlorine cars

Through the 1910s, chlorine and other pressurized goods were shipped in small tanks that were loaded aboard other freight cars; standard tank cars were only used for liquids not under

American Car & Foundry built this car for Solvay in 1934. It's a 5,800-gallon tank with a 40-ton capacity and a service platform and railing surrounding the bonnet. It has large manufacturer and commodity lettering. *Roy E. Meates*

Mathieson Chemicals leased this chlorine car from Shippers Car Line. The 40-ton, ICC 105A 300 car was built by American Car & Foundry in 1940. *American Car & Foundry*

From the 1930s through the 1960s, specially equipped flatcars (AAR class TMU) carried chlorine "ton containers" in built-in cradles on the deck; clamps secure the ends/rims of each cylinder. Each of the 15 cylinders weighs about 3,500 pounds loaded. The ACF car above is carrying loaded containers through Chicago in October 1960. *Above: J. David Ingles; below: American Car & Foundry*

pressure. The American Railway Association (ARA) released its first specifications for high-pressure tank cars in 1917. Class V cars were high-pressure cars with welded tanks and heavier shells than conventional non-pressurized cars. Chlorine was among the first commodities to travel in pressure tank cars.

In 1927 the Interstate Commerce Commission (ICC) assumed the role of classifying tank cars. The previous ARA V high-pressure tank car became the ICC-105. The pressure was eventually added to the specification, with a "W" following indicating a welded tank.

The first chlorine cars of the 1920s and 1930s were small because of the high density of the product. Cars 3,000, 4,000, and 6,000 gallons in

General American built this 10,500-gallon pressure car in 1952. It's leased to Wyandotte Chemicals and carrying chlorine. The 70-ton car has a coating of snow atop it in this 1962 view. *J. David Ingles*

size (30- or 40-ton capacity) were common. These cars often stood out in trains because of their small diameters compared to typical 8,000- and 10,000-gallon general purpose tank cars. Even after larger (10,500-gallon, 50-ton) cars began appearing in the 1940s, many smaller cars were built and remained in service into the 1960s and later, serving customers who didn't require larger shipments. Size is a spotting feature of chlorine cars, as they are much smaller than pressure cars carrying LPG or anhydrous ammonia, both of which have about half the density of chlorine.

Pressure cars have a welded interior tank with thick walls to withstand pressures at 300 to 500 psi. These tanks were insulated, with a thinner outer metal jacket that covered the insulating blanket. Pressure cars have no bottom outlets or steam lines; all product inlets, outlets, and valves are located in the housing ("bonnet") atop the car, which is smaller than the large expansion domes found on steam-era non-pressure cars. (See Chapter 6 on LPG for a detailed photo.)

Through the 1950s, tank cars had separate frames (center sills), with the tank strapped into saddles above each bolster and a running board along each side. Centered side ladders led to the housing; some cars have platforms with railings around the bonnet (this is usually at the owner's or lessor's option).

From the 1930s through the 1960s, chlorine was also sometimes transported in small containers— pressure tanks or cylinders—aboard specially equipped 42-foot flatcars. These tanks, standard in the chlorine industry, are known as "ton containers." They are 30" in diameter, 82" long, weigh 1,500 pounds unloaded, and as their name implies, hold 2,000 pounds of liquid chlorine under pressure.

The 42-foot flatcars carrying them held 15 of the containers in transverse saddles along the car. This meant a fully loaded weight of about 52,000 pounds in cylinders, plus the car weight of about 34,000 pounds, to carry just 15 tons of product. The cars were popular with smaller users, such as municipal water utilities, where containers could

MODELING TIP

Chlorine cars

Chlorine cars can appear in freight trains in any region of the country, en route from producer to consuming industry. They are generally single-car shipments, although you'll see strings of cars near chemical plants that produce chlorine. Atlas offers a modern ACF chlorine car in HO and N scale. Trix and BLI have made 6,000-gallon models of older-era framed cars in HO (typical of 1930s and 1940s cars), which would be appropriate operating through the 1970s. The old Athearn HO "chemical tank car" could stand in for a larger car from the 1940s-50s. A 3-D printed kit for a cylinder/flatcar has been made by DMS Engineering (offered through Shapeways.com), and brass models have been offered for that car, as well as many other types of tank cars.

Many early chlorine cars were noticeably smaller than other standard cars. This 3,100-gallon, 30-ton capacity car was built for Solvay in the late 1930s. It was repainted in 1956, and in this October 1960 view, it shows the old-style white placards with "DANGEROUS" and "CHLORINE" lettering. *J. David Ingles*

be sent to a central distributor and then trucked to multiple end users who only required smaller quantities.

These cars, class TMU, ran from the 1930s into the 1960s. Shippers Car Line (SHPX) leased them to many manufacturers; Diamond Alkali and Penn Salt were among private owners having their own cars.

Car evolution

As with other car types, chlorine tank cars grew as the standard weight limits rose to 100 tons (263K GRL) in the early 1960s. A major change in tank cars was the move to frameless tank cars by the early 1960s. Most new cars after that point use the tank body itself as the frame, with the tank welded to the bolsters at each end.

Cars of 16,800-gallon, 85-ton capacity were built in the early 1960s, but it was the ACF 17,360-gallon car that became the most common chlorine car in 1968 and later. Many smaller cars remained in service based on needs of end users. Other manufacturers were soon also building similar cars around 18,000-gallon capacity; the Trinity car on page 25 is a modern example. Along with the frameless style, these cars ride on roller-bearing trucks of various designs.

Car ownership and lettering

As with other tank cars, chlorine cars are privately owned, either by the shippers themselves (usually chemical companies) or by leasing companies such as Shippers Car Line (owned by ACF), Union (UTLX), and General American (GATX).

The heavy center sill and brake gear are clearly visible below the tank on this General American-built chlorine car owned by Hooker Chemicals. The 70-ton, ICC 105A 500W car, built in the 1950s, is insulated but lacks the end lip of many early insulated cars. It has received a Chemtrec label and contact number decal and consolidation stencils by this 1981 photo. *J. David Ingles*

The ACF 17,300-gallon, DOT 105J 500W tank car is a common modern chlorine carrier, with frameless design and roller-bearing trucks. It has a Chemtrec label and an inspection matrix, along with chlorine and inhalation hazmat placards. It was built in 1998. *Jeff Wilson*

Trinity built this 18,000-gallon DOT 105J 600I chlorine tank car in 2016. It includes "CHLORINE INHALATION HAZARD" stenciling and a pair of hazmat placards on each side and end. *Cody Grivno*

In an era dominated by mostly plain black tank cars, chlorine and other chemical cars often stood out for their colorful paint schemes. Through the 1960s, it was common for the name and logo of the owner or lessee of these cars to be prominently displayed on the side. This practice largely went away by the 1970s, and most modern chlorine cars are plain, with small lettering denoting the lessee.

A car in chlorine service will not be used for other commodities. As single-commodity hazardous-material cars, chlorine cars have stenciling for their lading on the right end of each side above the data. Lettering varies; examples include "CHLORINE," "LIQUID CHLORINE," or "CHLORINE LOADING ONLY." Larger lettering was added by some owners/lessees.

Diamond-shaped hazardous material placards are carried in brackets on each side and end of loaded cars. Early placards were not specific—white cards with "DANGEROUS" and "CHLORINE" lettering. Modern placards include the four-digit product (U.N.) code (1017 for chlorine) along with lettering (still on a white background).

Since 1998, cars carry information on tank and valve inspection and test dates in a matrix at the right end of each side. Cars also carry a contact number for emergencies.

Further information

An outstanding resource on early tank cars is Edward Kaminski's *Tank Cars: American Car & Foundry Company, 1865 to 1955* (Signature Press); other good books are James Kinkaid's *Tank Car Color Guide*, volumes 1 (early cars with center sills) and 2 (modern stub-sill cars), both by Morning Sun. A nice summary article of chlorine cars is "ACF 17,360-gallon Chlorine Tank Cars from Atlas HO and N scale Models," by Edward S. Kaminski, which appeared in *RailModel Journal* in December 2001.

CHAPTER THREE

Lumber

A Southern Pacific flatcar carries strapped bundles of Sierra Pacific 1 x 4s in 1993. Individual bundles are strapped, then bundles are banded together for stability. The standard 53-foot, 75-ton car was an unusual choice by this period, as bulkhead and center-beam cars had become the primary lumber haulers. *J. David Ingles*

Wood products, including dimensional lumber, milled shapes, plywood, and other sheet materials, are vital for construction across the continent. Railroads have always been a prime carrier of these goods, and currently move about 420,000 carloads of lumber annually. How railroads have carried this traffic has changed substantially since the steam era.

Through the 1950s, lumber loads were hand-stacked on flatcars. Large posts in the cars' stake pockets hold the loads; posts were tied together with planks or wire across the tops of the loads. This is on Union Pacific in the 1940s. *Union Pacific*

Most lumber in the U.S. is used for housing, so there is a close correlation between lumber traffic and the new-housing market. One modern center-beam car carries enough framing lumber to build five or six new houses.

Lumber is produced at sawmills throughout the U.S., with the majority in the Pacific Northwest and Southeast. Many areas in Canada also produce building products. Major companies include Weyerhaeuser, Georgia-Pacific, Sierra Pacific, Canfor, Potlatch, and RSG; many smaller companies and mills produce specialty products. Lumber products are also imported, arriving at coastal and Gulf ports.

Lumber-producing areas will see the highest concentration of rail traffic, with railcars going literally everywhere in the country. The final destination for lumber cars today is usually a large reload center or lumber distribution company that stores and reloads products onto trucks for final delivery to lumber yards and contractors. Through the 1960s, deliveries direct to lumber yards were common; small

Southern Pacific staged this photo in 1963 to show the then-innovative technique of bundling loads, which allows easy loading and unloading by forklift. The railroad also noted that bundling allowed larger loads: about 75,000 board-feet (bf) here, compared to about 42,000 bf for a hand-stacked load. *Southern Pacific*

towns and cities often had multiple lumber yards, which either had their own rail spurs or used team tracks. The shift in market since that time has eliminated many small dealers, although some larger lumber yards still receive rail shipments directly.

Types of lumber being shipped fall into a few categories. Dimensional lumber includes rough-cut and finished planks in various grades, kiln-dried, which can be treated or untreated.

Bulkhead flatcars provide increased load stability compared to standard flats. This 62-foot Mississippi & Skuna Valley car is loaded with rather loosely stacked bundles in 1980. *J. David Ingles*

Dimensional lumber for construction has always presented a challenge in transporting, as it's made in lengths from 8 to 16 feet, making it difficult to load in boxcars.

Plywood increased in popularity in the 1940s, and a variety of sheet materials are now common: particle board, MDF (medium-density fiberboard), OSB (oriented-strand board), and plasterboard (drywall); all require protection from the elements.

Through the 1950s, the typical method of shipping lumber was by hand-stacking it, either on a flatcar or—for high-grade untreated lumber that requires protection—in a boxcar. Both were labor-intensive.

Flatcars

Through the 1950s, standard flatcars were common for dimensional lumber loads not requiring protection from weather. Lumber was stacked board by board either directly on the car deck or on thin crosswise strips. As many stacks would be loaded as length allowed, with longer boards at the bottom and shorter boards on top; mixed loads were common.

Loads were secured by vertical posts in the car's stake pockets. The posts were tapered slightly at the bottom and sized to force-fit in the pockets. These posts would be secured across the top of the load by horizontal boards, wire, or cable, pulling the sides together and compressing downward on the stacks as much as possible to limit shifting.

By the 1970s, bundled loads were often wrapped to protect them. This 70-foot, 80-ton Burlington Northern bulkhead flatcar is carrying wrapped, bundled loads in the late 1980s. *Jeff Wilson collection*

Shifted loads were a problem with standard and bulkhead flats. Train motion has shifted and misaligned the lumber load significantly on this Apache car in 1969; it has been set out for restacking at Topeka, Kan. *J. David Ingles collection*

As you can imagine, along with being labor-intensive, this method did not secure the loads tightly. Boards were prone to shifting lengthwise during hard coupling or slack running in and out, and rocking motion could cause lateral misalignment, as well.

Gondolas were sometimes loaded in similar fashion, with vertical posts wedged between the lumber load and the inside walls of the car.

Flatcars with bulkheads, first widely used for pulpwood, began appearing in larger numbers in the 1940s and 1950s.

These became popular for lumber loads, as they contained extreme lengthwise shifting of loads. They were built in a wide variety of styles. A disadvantage was that the bulkheads added extra weight that took away from car capacity.

Standard 40-foot boxcars protected lumber loads well, but loading and unloading them stick-by-stick was time- and labor-intensive. *Clem Albers; Library of Congress*

Above: Double-door 50-foot boxcars became popular with lumber companies and railroads serving mills. Even though double-door cars made loading bundles of sheet materials easier, dimensional lumber—especially long planks—remained a challenge. *Steve Glischinski*

Left: Some boxcars were equipped with small inspection doors, often called "lumber doors," on one end. They offered some advantages for loading and unloading lumber, but were not an ideal solution. *Milwaukee Road*

Arcata & Mad River, owned by Simpson Lumber Co., had 100 double-door cars with 16-foot-wide openings and cushioning, built in 1978. *Jeff Wilson collection*

Pullman-Standard built 200 all-door boxcars for Southern in 1961-1962. Although designed for auto parts, they also carried lumber. The roll-up doors and moveable posts allowed an unobstructed 50-foot-wide opening for loading. Although initially successful, the doors proved to be prone to damage, and the design was not repeated.

Top: J. David Ingles collection; above: Southern Ry.

The advent of bundled lumber in the early 1960s was a major change. Dimensional lumber was stacked tightly at the mill and secured by metal banding. The stacks were then loaded and unloaded with forklifts, speeding the process. Banding keeps individual boards from shifting longitudinally. A Southern Pacific news release with the photo on page 27 noted that stacked lumber also allowed larger loads because of more efficient use of space.

Side stakes were no longer needed to hold loads in place on flatcars. Bundles were stacked with wood-strip spacers between them and further banded together to increase the stability of the load. These bundles were often stamped with logos of their producing mills.

Although bundled lumber greatly improved efficiency, loads could still shift sideways, as shown by the photo of the Apache flatcar on page 29. Cars with shifted loads were switched out of trains and restacked.

Bundling also allowed the use of plastic sheeting to create wrapped lumber bundles, protecting untreated dimensional and sheet products. These wraps are distinctive, with colorful logos and lettering reflecting the manufacturers and products.

Even with the introduction of center-beam cars, bundled lumber often traveled on conventional flatcars through the 1980s. Although they've become rare, lumber loads can still be found on standard bulkhead flats today.

Boxcars

Prior to wrapped bundles, boxcars were the only option for dimensional and sheet lumber that required protection from the elements. Lumber could be

Thrall built this Duluth & Northeastern (Potlatch) all-door car in 1973. It has the manufacturer's most-common 50'-6" interior length. Thrall cars have four Youngstown plug doors. *R.J. Wilhelm; J. David Ingles collection*

Any two doors can be opened at one time on all-door cars, allowing forklifts to efficiently load long stacks of dimensional lumber. *Thrall*

loaded in any common 40- or 50-foot, 50-ton boxcar. As with flatcars, lumber was loaded a board at a time ("stick by stick"), usually through the side door, a laborious, slow task.

Some steam-era boxcars had small inspection doors located high on one end. Often called "lumber doors," these could be used to load and unload

boards as well—easier than using the doors for long planks, but still a tedious process.

There was no way to get bundled lumber into boxcars with six-foot doors. In the 1960s, railroads carrying a lot of lumber began investing in 50-foot cars with double doors, especially to carry bundles of sheet

material (most of which measured 4x8 feet). Shorter lengths of dimensional lumber could also be loaded, as the photo on page 30 shows, but standard boxcars were still not the ideal solution. Double-door cars are still often used for lumber sheet materials.

All-door boxcars

The ideal solution appeared to be a boxcar, but with extra-wide door openings—some the full length of the car—to allow easier loading of long dimensional bundles. The first were built in 1961 by Pullman-Standard for the Southern. This car had a 51-foot interior length and three roll-up doors on each side, with moveable door posts, allowing a clear 50-foot-wide opening. Although designed for auto parts, they were also used for lumber.

The Southern eventually owned 200 of the cars, but unfortunately they were not successful. The car and frame allowed enough twisting to throw the doors out of alignment, and they proved to be unreliable in service.

The next attempt at an all-door car was an experimental version built by International (which was best known for building cabooses) for McCloud River in 1962. Although International didn't follow through with production models, the design showed enough

Early SIECO all-door cars closely resemble Thrall cars, with Youngstown doors. SIECO built this car in 1973; it's owned by U.S. Leasing (a giveaway that it's a SIECO car) and leased to Canadian Forest Products. This view is from 1976. *J. David Ingles collection*

The Evans Side Slider has two plug doors (middle) and two Superior sliding doors (left and right). Evans built this 70-ton Cooperstown & Charlotte Valley car in 1978; it's shown in September 1979. *R.J. Wilhelm; J. David Ingles collection*

promise that other manufacturers began offering similar cars.

The most common was the Thrall design, which it marketed as the "Thrall Door" car, built starting in 1967. Unlike standard boxcars, which rely in part on the sides for strength, all-door cars had heavy frames and ends. All-door cars are essentially bulkhead flatcars with a roof, which carried the side doors as a load. This meant these cars were heavy: A Thrall-Door car weighed around 76,000

pounds, about 15,000 pounds heavier than a standard 50-foot double-door boxcar.

Thrall's cars can be spotted by their four Youngstown sliding plug doors on each side. Two doors could be open at any given time, allowing access to half of the car at a time for loading. The Thrall cars have a slightly arched, smooth roof. Early versions had a 51'-8" interior length. Of the four side doors, three were standard 12-foot-wide Youngstown doors and

one (on the right as you look at the car side) was a non-standard 14-footer. The design was soon revised to use all 12-foot doors, which cut the car length to 50'-6". Most cars feature the shorter length.

The other common all-door car was made by Southern Iron & Equipment Co. (SIECO). The first were quite similar to the Thrall car, initially 49'-6" long (inside) but then stretched to 52'-5". Early versions also used four Youngstown plug doors, but with a

This is an early "opera window" 60-foot center-beam car built by Thrall for Burlington Northern in 1983. The cables are connected at angles on empty cars to keep them from dangling over the sides. *Jeff Wilson*

peaked roof and different end design from the Thrall car.

When Evans acquired SIECO in the 1970s, it redesigned the car by using less-expensive Superior (non-plug) sliding doors in the end positions. Evans called this car the Side Slider, and its appearance is distinctive. Pacific Car & Foundry also built a limited number of all-door cars (for Weyerhaeuser/Columbia & Cowlitz).

All-door cars were AAR class LU, and were owned and leased by railroads as well as lumber companies. Although they worked reasonably well, they were heavy and expensive, and the door mechanisms were maintenance-intensive, especially as the cars aged. Some were built as late as 1980, but the coming of the center-beam car doomed all-door cars, and most were out of service by the 2000s.

Center-beam flatcars

The center-beam flatcar revolutionized rail lumber traffic. Thrall built the first one in 1977. The design is basically a long bulkhead flatcar (center-beams have an inside length of either 60 or 73 feet), with a tall beam that runs lengthwise down the middle of the car. A series of built-in cables with hooks on winches line the side sill. When lumber bundles are loaded, the cables wrap over the lumber and hook to the beam, securing the load; no separate cables are needed. Bundles rest on a series of shallow transverse beams on the car deck, which are canted slightly inward to keep the loads stable.

The beam provides most of the car's structural strength, allowing for a light center sill and frame. This makes for a light car—about 63,000 pounds for a truss-design 73-foot car—giving an increased capacity compared to a standard flatcar or boxcar.

By the late 1980s, center-beams (AAR class FBC) had become the most-common method of transporting lumber, including dimensional as well as sheet materials. Wrapped bundles protect untreated and sensitive loads, while treated bundles are often unwrapped.

Several manufacturers have built center-beams, which feature two basic designs: "opera window" and truss. The so-called opera window cars came first. They have the center beam supported by vertical posts, with the space between posts filled by steel sheet with

A 73-foot Thrall truss-style car owned by TTX is being loaded in 1995. Cars must be loaded and unloaded evenly on each side. The transverse floor supports and vertical beams angle inward, helping to stabilize loads. *J. David Ingles collection*

Gunderson built this 73-foot truss-style center beam for Grand Trunk Western. It's carrying a load of non-wrapped dimensional lumber in the early 2000s. *Jeff Wilson*

This TTZX 73-foot center-beam carries a load of Georgia Pacific wrapped sheet material in 2007. The cables and top corner protectors are clearly visible against the white wrapping. *Jeff Wilson*

large oval holes. Thrall and Gunderson both offered 60-foot versions and then 73-foot versions; Thrall's design had ovals of the same size, while Gunderson cars had end openings that were smaller, plus a different car-end design.

In the late 1980s, builders moved to lighter truss-style designs. Gunderson, Trinity, and NSC cars have diagonals that cross in the middle panel. Gunderson's end diagonals terminate halfway up the end bulkhead; Trinity's and NSC's go to the top of the vertical post next to the bulkhead. Thrall's design has filled-in end panels, with

a pair of diagonals extending upward and outward on each side of the center section.

Loading and unloading is by forklift. Warning stencils on the cars remind operators to load and unload each side of the car evenly to avoid tipping. Loading and unloading areas at mills and distributors typically have track in an open area with paved or smooth gravel areas on each side.

Typically, 60-foot cars carry green lumber, plasterboard, and other heavy, high-density goods, with the longer (and more common) 73-footers carrying finished lumber and plywood.

Further information

The book *Model Realistic Freight Car Loads* by Keith Kohlmann has a chapter on modeling lumber, timber, and building-material loads. Morning Sun has several volumes in its *Open Top Loads* series of books, with lots of photos that will help in modeling.

CHAPTER FOUR

Cement

Two-bay covered hoppers have been the standard car for hauling cement since the 1930s. Greenville built this 2,003-cf, 70-ton car for Ann Arbor in 1964. It features welded construction and round roof hatches. Note the "FOR CEMENT LOADING ONLY ..." stenciling at left. *John Ingles; J. David Ingles collection*

Railroads have been carrying cement since the 1800s and still haul a great deal of it—about 210,000 carloads annually. Shipping methods have changed significantly, from bags of cement loaded in boxcars to covered hoppers of increasing size that allow the product to be carried in bulk. Cement was one of the first commodities commonly carried in covered hoppers in the 1930s.

Cement was commonly shipped in 94-pound bags through the 1940s. Because of its high density, a full load in a standard 50-ton boxcar was only about four feet high. A worker is unloading a car in California in 1940.

Russell Lee, Library of Congress

Portland cement (named for a region in England), developed in the early 1800s, is the most common type, accounting for about 95 percent of cement produced. Its main ingredient is limestone, plus clay and sand. It is made in huge rotary kilns.

Cement is the key ingredient in concrete. Note that cement and concrete are not the same: cement is an ingredient in concrete, which is one of the world's most-common building materials. Cement is a dense, fine powder. It's extremely heavy; a cubic foot of Portland cement weighs 94 pounds.

The U.S. used more than 100 million metric tons of cement in 2021, with much of it produced domestically; 96 plants produce about 90 million tons annually. The first U.S. cement plants began operating in the 1870s, and they are now located across the U.S., with many plants in the Northeast and the Midwest down through Texas.

Railroads play a key role in shipping cement. The typical distribution channel is for the cement manufacturing plant to use railroad cars to ship the product long distances, usually to a local distributor. The distributor then uses bulk tractor-trailers to ship cement to concrete batch plants. Cement plants also ship some product directly by truck, barge, and ship, and railroads carry cement to and from ports for import and export.

Because cement is a product used everywhere, cement cars can be found in trains along virtually every rail line. More cars will obviously be found on lines that have on-line (or nearby) cement plants. Railroads that have historically carried a great deal of cement traffic (and have owned a lot of cement cars) include Lehigh Valley, Lehigh & New England, Delaware, Lackawanna & Western, Minneapolis & St. Louis, New York Central, and Pennsylvania.

Shipping

Cement requires careful handling, as it is easily contaminated by moisture (direct contact with water or excess humidity). When exposed to water, it clumps and becomes hard, rendering it unusable. It needs to be stored in a waterproof environment—either in sealed bags or in watertight bulk tanks or containers. This has always made transporting cement a challenge.

In the early days of railroading, cement was shipped in wooden barrels. Although these barrels ranged in capacity from 265 to 400 pounds, the standard eventually became barrels holding four cubic feet of cement (376

American Car & Foundry built this Delaware & Hudson gondola and air-activated cement containers in 1942 (above). They are the later-version 11-ton containers. The openings in the gondola sides allowed access for hoses for unloading. The container at left is an earlier 10-ton version. *Two photos: American Car & Foundry*

pounds). This became the measurement that, although obsolete with the demise of the barrels themselves, remained a standard unit in the industry until 1972. Cement is now measured in short tons (2,000 pounds).

Barrels gave way to bags by about 1900. Heavy cloth bags came first, followed by reinforced paper bags. They remained the common method of shipping through the 1940s. Each standard bag weighs 94 pounds (one cubic foot), making it easy to measure the amount used. These bags carried the logos and names of the producers, often with colorful graphics. Although bags are still produced for single-consumer use, all other cement is transported in bulk.

Ready-mix plants serving construction companies and others account for about two-thirds of cement

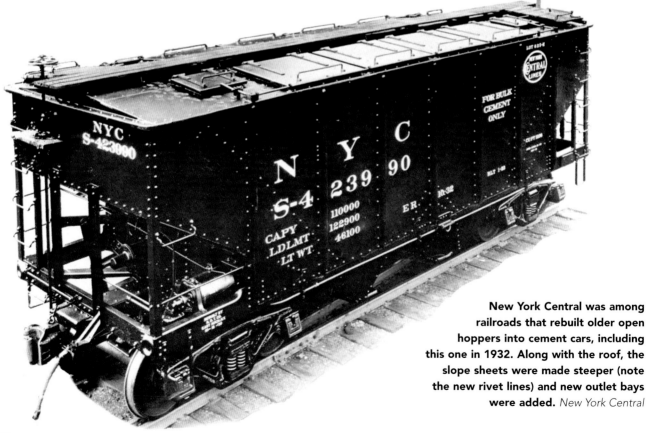

New York Central was among railroads that rebuilt older open hoppers into cement cars, including this one in 1932. Along with the roof, the slope sheets were made steeper (note the new rivet lines) and new outlet bays were added. *New York Central*

Greenville manufactured the first true purpose-built cement covered hoppers, a 50-car lot for Erie in 1934. The 1,321-cf cars had a capacity of 50 tons. TRAINS *magazine collection*

produced, with producers of concrete products using about 14 percent. The rest goes to consumer use, highway contractors, and other end users.

Railcars

Standard boxcars were the original method of shipping cement by rail, first in barrels, then in bags from about 1900 through the 1940s. Loading and unloading were labor-intensive and time-consuming. Loads were easy to calculate: a 50-ton boxcar could carry 1,060 sacks of cement. Although this sounds like a lot, it didn't come close to filling a car; the bags were only loaded to about a third of the car interior height (see the photo on page 37).

The ultimate solution was transporting cement in bulk. Open hopper cars obviously weren't the answer, nor was simply loading it in bulk form into a boxcar (as was done with grain). Railroads approached the challenge in two ways: by loading cement in containers that could be

American Car & Foundry and Lehigh & New England developed a popular design for a 70-ton, 1,790-cf cement car in 1937. That and similar 1,958-cf versions would become popular cement cars through the 1940s. *American Car & Foundry*

Pennsylvania's 70-ton, 1,973-cf class H30 cement cars were distinctive, with their three bays, angled braces at the ends, and long, low appearance. Number 254259 was built in 1935 and shown here in 1961. *John Ingles, J. David Ingles collection*

 **MODELING TIP**

Covered hopper models

A wide variety of two-bay covered hopper models have been produced, including resin and brass models of several early railroad-built cars. 3D-printed models of air-activated containers and whale-belly covered hoppers have been offered by several vendors through Shapeways (shapeways.com). Older cars typically had long service lives, usually about 40 years from their built dates. The cement causes cars to weather uniquely, and a gray-streaked, dusty, rusted appearance is common for older cars.

Cement cars can be found on trains throughout the country, heading from cement plants to distributors. These historically have not been long hauls, as it's not worth shipping the product into another manufacturer's territory. Thus cars of cement-carrying railroads rarely go farther than 600-800 miles from their home plants unless there are no closer cement plants.

New York Central's two-bay Enterprise covered hoppers had angled posts on the end side panels and 10 square roof hatches. This 70-ton, 1,800-cf car was built in 1940. *TRAINS magazine collection*

loaded on and off railcars and trucks, and by adding covers to hopper cars. Although this would be the ultimate solution, it would take a few years to perfect the concept.

Cement containers

Since the 1910s, the LCL Corporation (a New York Central subsidiary) had been operating small shipping containers that could be loaded in gondolas and transloaded to trucks. By the late 1920s, these included bulk containers for powdered lime, a material similar to cement. The rectangular containers each held six tons and were loaded and unloaded by gravity. They had to be removed from their gondola to unload the product.

In the early 1930s, LCL Corp. contracted with American Car & Foundry to build a new design of air-activated containers to carry cement. These were vertical cylinders with a loading hatch on top and a tapered bottom with an unloading port. They

Baltimore & Ohio built several classes of round-roof covered hoppers used for cement. This class N-34 car, built in 1940, has a 70-ton, 1,700-cf capacity. *TRAINS magazine collection*

used compressed air to unload, which forced the product through the outlet port. This allowed the containers to be unloaded via hoses while they remained in the car.

Early containers held 10 tons of cement and were typically carried six per gondola; later versions held 11 tons and were carried five per gondola. The gondolas had four or five rectangular openings on each side to allow access for the air and discharge hoses. Many gondolas were built by AC&F: 70-ton capacity cars with a 46'-3" interior length and interior guides to hold the containers in position during transit. Some railroads rebuilt existing gons for the service. A six-container car could be unloaded in about an hour and a half.

These "bottle cars" were used in the Northeast. Owners included Delaware & Hudson; Delaware, Lackawanna & Western; Lehigh Valley; and New York Central. Some survived in service into the 1960s. A key reason for their continued service long after covered hoppers were in wide use was delivering cement to New York City, because it was preferable in car-float operations to use container cars, then transfer the containers to trucks, as opposed to floating covered hoppers

and having to transload bulk cement to trucks.

Covered hoppers

In the 1920s into the 1930s, railroads and manufacturers were experimenting with putting covers on standard (open) hopper cars to protect sensitive lading. Phosphate cars were among the first in the 1920s, and by the early 1930s twin-bay coal hoppers refitted with roofs and

hatches were being used for cement.

These cars were not ideal. The slope sheets of a standard hopper were not steep enough to allow cement to readily empty; bottom outlet gates designed for coal didn't stop fine powder from leaking; and the end design made it difficult to fill the ends of the cars with a roof added. Although some railroads would rebuild open hoppers in this fashion through the

Pullman-Standard's popular cement hopper of the 1940s was this 1,958-cf, 70-ton car. Like ACF's car, the PS car had angled cutouts on each side. This car was built for Minneapolis & St. Louis in 1947. *Minneapolis & St. Louis*

Pullman-Standard's PS-2 design introduced all-welded construction and round roof hatches. This 100-ton version, built in 1964 for Detroit & Mackinac, has a 2,600-cf capacity. *John Ingles, J. David Ingles collection*

ACF applied its Center Flow design to two-bay cars starting in the mid-1960s. This 100-ton, 2,970-cf has the original early body with single horizontal stiffener along the upper side. *Jeff Wilson collection*

1940s, the best solution was a purpose-built cement car.

The first covered hoppers built new for cement appeared in 1934, an order of 50 two-bay cars built by Greenville for the Erie. The two-bay car had a capacity of 1,321 cubic feet, with a nominal 50-ton capacity. It had steep slope sheets, bottom outlets with flat plates to better contain the contents and make unloading easier, and eight large, square roof hatches. The density of cement required a car smaller than a coal hopper (a USRA open hopper of 1920 was 1,880 cf as built).

Other cars soon appeared, with American Car & Foundry and Pullman-Standard building most cement cars through the 1940s. Both offered slightly larger (1,790- and 1,958-cf) 70-ton cars. These originally had open angled cutouts above the side sills between the middle slope sheets; on later cars, the spaces were filled.

Several railroads also built cars to their own designs. The Pennsylvania built more than 1,500 class H30 and H30a cars from 1935 to 1952. These 70-ton cars were distinctive: longer and lower than other cement covered

hoppers, with three bays and angled end bracing. New York Central's Enterprise covered hoppers were also easy to spot. They looked like a conventional two-bay covered hopper, but had inward-facing angled posts on each end panel. They were also 70-ton cars.

Baltimore & Ohio built several series of cement covered hoppers with a rounded "wagon-top" design also used on its home-built boxcars. The sides wrapped around to the roof, giving them a unique appearance. The first (class N-31) in 1935 were 50-ton cars; later series (classes N-34, -38, and -40), built into the 1940s, were 70-ton cars.

Pullman-Standard introduced a brand-new design in 1952 with its PS-2 line of welded covered hoppers. The first cement cars were 2,003-cf, 70-ton cars, and by the early 1960s PS was building larger 2,600-cf, 100-ton versions. These had eight vertical side posts (four on each end with a gap in the middle) and introduced round roof hatches, which provided a better seal than the older square hatches.

Other builders followed shortly with similar designs, including Greenville and ACF. In spotting these cars, look at the overall size (length, height, and cubic capacity), number

New York Central's Flexi-Flo cars, built by ACF, were the first pressure-differential covered hoppers. The 125-ton car is transloading cement to a truck trailer in 1965. *New York Central*

The Greenville 3,000-cf two-bay covered hopper was a popular 100-ton car design. This Union Pacific car was built in 1984. *Jeffrey Torretta*

and style of side posts, shape and design of the end slope sheets, and the pattern and design of the end bracing, ladders, and side sills.

Modern cars

The early 1960s saw the move to larger 100-ton cars. "Jumbo" covered hoppers for grain service began appearing

General American's Pressure Slide was a tank-style pressure-differential car with a single bottom outlet. This Chicago, Burlington & Quincy car was built in 1967 and shown serving Burlington Northern in 1978.
R.J. Wilhelm, J. David Ingles collection

Union introduced a tank-style pressure car in 1967 called the Pressure-Flow. This is one of 50 3,000-cf cars initially leased to Dundee Cement. It has three outlets connected to a common discharge pipe. *UTLX*

North American's pressure-differential cars have distinct angled ends. This 2,785-cf car is carrying fly ash—a common concrete ingredient—but similar cars are used for cement. *Jeff Wilson*

in large numbers, but cement cars remained smaller, still with two bays. The biggest design change was ACF's introduction of the Center Flow design (discussed in Chapter 1). For cement, this meant cars of 2,970 cf capacity. Several other builders were soon building 100-ton exterior-post cars at or near 3,000 cf, including PS, Greenville, and Portec.

The mid-1960s saw the introduction of pressure-differential covered hoppers. These cars used air pressure from a trackside source to force lading out of the car. The first was New York Central's Flexi-Flow cars in 1964, built by ACF. The cars were heavy: 125-ton capacity (315,000-pound GRL), designed for on-line use. They were designed for direct transloading of cement to semi trailers.

Trinity built this 110-ton (286K GRL), 3,281-cf car for CSX in 2011. It shares the same roof style and other spotting features of the company's larger grain covered hoppers. *Cody Grivno*

This NSC 3,220-cf car was built in 2009 and photographed in 2014. *Cody Grivno*

Further information

The book *The Model Railroader's Guide to Industries Along the Tracks Vol. 3* by Jeff Wilson (Kalmbach, 2008) includes a chapter on the cement industry, including history, manufacturing, plant layout, and railroad operations.

General American introduced a tank-style pressure-differential covered hopper called the Pressure Slide in 1967. The 100-ton, 2,800-cf covered car had a low-slung center (they were nicknamed "whale belly" cars). A total of 100 were built (50 each for Burlington and Seaboard Air Line).

Union offered a similar car in 1967, the tank-style Pressure-Flow car. The first were 3,000-cf cars with three bottom outlets feeding a common outlet pipe. About 250 were built, all in the UTLX fleet; 2,800-, 3,500-, 3,800-, and 4,000-cf cars were also built.

North American built a pressure-differential car that was popular for cement and many other commodities. The PD3000 (2,785 cf) and PD4000 (3,900 cf) cars had a cylindrical cross-section with boxed-in, angled ends. Pressure-differential cars are marked by piping running along the outlet bays.

Car size increased again with the move to 286K GRL (110-ton) cars in 1995. Most cars after this point have been built with the curved-side design pioneered by ACF. Spotting features are largely the same for these as their larger grain-carrying siblings (see Chapter 1), with cars made by ACI, Gunderson/Greenbrier, NSC, and Trinity.

CR 606669

CAPY 200000 GBS
LD LMT 205200 CR-BL
LT WT 57800 7 ·81

CHAPTER FIVE

Coil steel

Pennsylvania Railroad's class G41A cars were among the first dedicated cars for carrying coil steel. The 100-ton cars have transverse cradles. This one, built in 1968, is carrying four hot-rolled coils for successor Conrail in 1984. Rust patterns under the end cradles show where hot coils have scorched away paint. *J. David Ingles*

Since the 1950s, the most common way of getting sheet metal from mills to manufacturers is in rolls of coiled steel— known in the industry simply as "coil steel." Coil steel is a long piece of sheet steel that has been tightly wound into a roll. Railroads initially shipped coil steel in gondolas, then in special-purpose coil steel cars starting in the 1960s.

The Pennsylvania Railroad converted this 70-ton, 52-foot mill gondola to coil steel service in 1955 by adding cradle-style floor skids and a pair of removable sheet-steel hoods. *TRAINS magazine collection*

The auto industry is the largest customer for coil steel, using it to stamp a wide variety of body parts and panels. Coil steel is also used in a tremendous variety of other products, including appliances, containers (tin and aluminum cans), construction materials (roof and wall panels), and innumerable other consumer products and components—anything that can be stamped from a sheet of steel or other metal.

Coils gained in popularity because they're easy to handle and transport without damage compared to large, flat sheets, especially for thin stock. Steel is the most common material, but other types of metal, such as aluminum and brass, are also available in coils.

Steel mills roll coils of various metallurgical composition based on the needs of users. The finished coils are made to the customer's size specifications, including thickness, width, length, and weight. End users use decoilers, which hold the coils under tension while unrolling and flattening the material.

Coil steel falls into two broad categories: hot rolled and cold rolled. Hot-rolled steel is rolled at high temperature, with the process producing a rough, oxidized surface. It's used in situations where the finish isn't important. Hot-rolled coils are sometimes still extremely hot when they're loaded in cars; you can see on

Skids with V-shaped cradles were placed in gondolas to carry coils. The cross brackets could be adjusted to any coil width to secure them and keep them from sliding. *Nickel Plate Road*

some cars where paint and lettering have melted and run (with missing paint and rust) because of the coils' heat (see the Pennsy car on page 46).

Cold-rolled steel is further processed and re-rolled (often at a separate mill), with oxidation removed and the surface milled to the desired finish. This means cold-rolled steel is more expensive and more susceptible to damage, so it's always shipped with covers to protect it.

Hot-rolled steel doesn't require this level of protection, so if you see open rolls of steel, it's hot-rolled, either on its way to a final user or en route to a mill that produces cold-rolled steel. These rolls will often have a visible coating of oxidation or light rust.

Coils require care in handling. They are heavy—individual coils weigh from 5 to 25 tons—and are handled by overhead cranes or forklifts with special cradles. The size and weight

Evans coil gondola

The problem of misplaced hoods on coil cars led to this distinctive Evans car, built in November 1967. It's a gondola specifically for handling coils, with a built-in cover comprising two sections that rotate to the sides for loading and unloading. Evans called it an "integral cover coil car," and it was nicknamed a clamshell or breadbox car. A total of 60 were built: 50 for Pittsburgh & Lake Erie and 10 for Bethlehem & Lake Erie. They were high-capacity 125-ton cars, with a 315K GRL.

The design wasn't successful. They were heavy (three tons heavier than a 125-ton coil car), and the covers were often damaged in mills—sometimes by operators unfamiliar with the cars who improperly used cranes to try to remove them. The cars were rebuilt starting in 1973, with the covers removed and removable hoods added, but they could still be spotted by the pair of rounded vertical door tracks on each side, which remained after rebuilding.

Three-month-old Pittsburgh & Lake Erie no. 42289 rolls on a train in February 1968 (above). The roof halves are rolled to the sides (below) to allow loading and unloading.
Above: John Ingles, J. David Ingles collection; below: Pittsburgh & Lake Erie

New York Central 749938 is one of 100 gondolas built by the railroad in 1962 specifically for hauling hot-rolled coils (no hoods required). Note the braced ends, which served as an end stop for the coil load. It's shown in 1964.
John Ingles, J. David Ingles collection

of each coil is based on what the end customer needs. For example, if the customer's crane and decoiler are rated at 15 tons, it won't receive coils heavier than that. See "Calculating coil sizes and weight" on page 52 for information on coil specifics.

Coils are held together by multiple bands of steel strap. Common damage comes from dropping the coils or setting them down too hard, which can knock them out of round, meaning they won't fit into a decoiling machine. They can also be damaged by sliding or hitting them from the side, which can mar the surface and/or cause coils to partially spiral out.

Gondolas

Railroads began hauling coil steel by the 1930s, but it wasn't until the mid to late 1950s that the business grew to the point that large numbers of cars were needed for the service. The coils' shape and weight made it difficult to carry them on a standard flat or gondola without modification. They were usually handled lying flat, but that made loading and unloading difficult; they needed to be on a pallet or flat rack to enable them to be lifted.

In the early 1950s, railroads began outfitting mill gondolas for dedicated coil service. This was done by adding shallow V-shaped channels lengthwise

Railroads still use gondolas to carry coils. These Indiana Harbor Belt mill gons (stenciled "COIL LOADING ONLY") are carrying hot-rolled coils in 1991. The lettering has been distorted by heat from the coils. *J. David Ingles*

Chesapeake & Ohio in 1963 built coil car No. 82000 by cutting down the sides and ends of a mill gon, rebuilding the floor with a trough, and adding cushioning. It served as the prototype for future purpose-built coil cars.
John Ingles, J. David Ingles collection

down the center of the car, creating a cradle (skid) that held the coils in position. The cradles were lined with hardwood to provide a surface that wouldn't mar the metal.

The Nickel Plate Road in 1955 applied for a patent on the gondola skid shown on page 47, which was approved in 1959. It has two cradles end to end, with spring-loaded buffers secured inside each car end. This allowed the skids to slide on the floor to absorb shocks, as gondolas of the era were rarely fitted with cushioning devices. Early cars simply used canvas covers, but removable steel hoods soon became the standard method of protecting loads.

Mill gondolas (52-foot) were the most common for this. Cars thus converted are listed in the *Official*

Purpose-built coil cars, like Pennsylvania's class G41 cars of 1965, made more efficient use of space than gondolas. The 100-ton car had a 38'-6" inside length and weighed 64,000 pounds. *Pennsylvania Railroad*

Detroit, Toledo & Ironton no. 1051 is an Evans Type 3 coil car, shown just after it was built in 1967. The 100-ton car has a slight fishbelly side sill, side running boards, and a Hydra-Cushion underframe (its hydraulic reservoir is visible projecting downward below the middle of the car). *John Ingles, J. David Ingles collection*

Coil cars have permanent troughs, lined with wood (as this car) or a cushioned coating over steel. The bulkheads are adjustable and lock in place along the trough to hold coils in position. *John Ingles; J. David Ingles collection*

Railway Equipment Register (ORER) as such, and are classified GBS, with "GB" indicating a mill gondola and the "S" a built-in rack for specialized service. By the early 1960s, railroads rostering these cars included Chesapeake & Ohio; Detroit, Toledo & Ironton; Elgin, Joliet & Eastern; Grand Trunk Western; New York Central; Nickel Plate Road; Pennsylvania; Pittsburgh & Lake Erie; and Reading. All of these railroads served steel mill and auto industry regions.

An advantage of using standard mill gons with skids is that it was relatively easy to add and remove the cradles/skids as needed, so if coil traffic fell, gondolas could be converted back to standard mill service. The increase in coil traffic in the 1960s led some railroads to build gondolas (or rebuild old ones) with permanent cradles to handle coils.

Although gondolas worked well, they were far from ideal. With the 52-foot length of mill gons, a full load of coils usually didn't come close to completely filling the space before maxing out the 70-ton load limit. The gon sides and ends (and the full floor below the cradles) added a lot of dead (tare) weight that wasn't needed, cutting down on the potential payload that could be carried.

The eventual answer was the commodity-specific coil car, but some gondolas remained—and still remain—in service carrying coil steel, especially for peak traffic periods.

Early coil cars

The move to 100-ton (263,000-pound gross rail load) cars as the interchange standard in 1963, along with a growing traffic base for coil steel, led railroads and manufacturers to look for more efficient methods of carrying the product.

Among the first was Chesapeake & Ohio, which in 1963 rebuilt a 1940s-era 52-foot mill gondola by cutting down the sides and ends, adding

underframe cushioning and roller-bearing trucks, and fitting it with a permanent center trough for coils. The 263K GRL car was heavy, with a light weight of 93,000 pounds, but proved the worth of the design. The railroad then built 100 cars in its Raceland shops (plus 100 for Baltimore & Ohio) in 1964. The production cars were shorter (50'-3" inside length) and lighter, giving them a higher load limit than the initial car.

MODELING TIP

Coil cars

Atlas, ExactRail, InterMountain, ScaleTrains, Tangent, and Walthers have offered coil car models; also check vendors on Shapeways.com—several offer coil car, coil, and hood models. Hoods swapped among early coil cars was common, making it easy to model unique cars. You'll see more of the cars in trains serving steel mills and auto plants, but they run across the country as single cars or in small groups.

This Elgin, Joliet & Eastern car is an Evans Type 4, built in 1975—note the straight side sills. By 1979, both original hoods were gone, with a Chessie System round and Norfolk & Western angled hood in their place. *J. David Ingles*

Evans built some 125-ton coil cars (315K GRL), including this Pittsburgh & Lake Erie car, in 1966. They were about five feet longer than Evans' 100-ton car. *John Ingles, J. David Ingles collection*

Thrall built this 100-ton coil car for Chicago & North Western in 1969. It has straight side sills with a small channel extension jutting out above each bolster. *Thrall*

This Norfolk & Western class F-42 coil car was built by FMC in 1967. It has fishbelly side sills and distinctive rounded hoods with vertical corrugations. *John Ingles, J. David Ingles collection*

Calculating coil sizes and weight

One of the best ways to determine the size and weight of a steel coil is an online calculator provided by Steel Warehouse, a steel product distributor. You can find it at www.steelwarehouse.com/steel-coil-calculators/. Other companies and websites offer similar calculators.

The Pennsylvania Railroad and Evans Products Co. both introduced dedicated coil cars in 1964. The Pennsy built a single car (class G40), no. 387000, as a test, then followed it with 87 class G41 cars and another 238 class G41a cars through 1968, all built at its Samuel Rea shops. The cars were unique compared to later coil cars in having troughs transverse to the deck. The 100-ton capacity cars had an inside length of 38'-6" and were 46 feet long overall. A pair of steel, angled-top hoods covered three troughs, and the cars used Pullman-Standard 60"-travel cushion underframes. Most survived through the Conrail era.

The Evans car differed by having a lengthwise cradle, with multiple transverse bulkheads/brackets that could be adjusted and locked to hold coils of any width in position. The 100-ton cars were welded, were longer (45'-6") inside than the PRR cars, had

Whitehead & Kales built 200 coil cars for Detroit, Toledo & Ironton in 1967. They had fishbelly side sills, bolt heads marking the cross-bearer locations, and rounded hoods with horizontal corrugations. *John Ingles, J. David Ingles collection*

fishbelly side sills (sill deeper in the middle than over the trucks), and were cushioned.

Most dedicated coil cars are classified as flatcars (FMS), although the Pennsy classified its G41 car as a gondola (GBSR).

The Evans car became the most popular design into the 1970s and was purchased by a number of railroads. The first cars became known as Type 1 versions. The design was soon stretched to a 48'-0" inside length (Type 2). In 1967, side running boards were added (Type 3), and in 1968, the car design changed to have straight

side sills in a channel style with a pair of vertical stiffeners on each side. This version (Type 4) became the most common Evans car and was built through the 1970s.

Hood styles varied, with rounded or angled (smooth-sided) tops. Hoods became problematic for railroads. Since they were removable, they sometimes didn't get replaced on a car after unloading, or were placed back on the wrong car. As the photos throughout this chapter show, it wasn't unusual for cars to have one or both hoods from railroads different than the car owner.

A notable car variation built by

Evans was a 125-ton car (315,000-pound GRL) built primarily for Pittsburgh & Lake Erie (250 cars) but also for Bethlehem & Lake Erie (15). The cars were longer than the 100-ton version (53'-4" inside length) and were restricted on their routes.

Evans also furnished its cars as kits, and identical cars were built by some railroads under license.

Thrall became a major builder of coil cars as well. Its 52'-1" length cars resembled the Evans Type 4 design, with a deep, straight side sill, but had projections above the bolster ends above each truck.

Conrail's CoilShield cars, built by Thrall, have coils riding in a well between the trucks with a unique one-piece hood design. This car, built in 1993, went to CSX after the CR breakup (as evidenced by the NYC reporting marks). *Jeff Wilson*

Johnstown America's 110-ton coil cars have channel-style side sills with vertical stiffeners and a slight fishbelly drop in the middle. The hood has a noticeably different curve compared to those on other cars. *Jeff Wilson*

FMC built coil cars that resembled the Evans fishbelly design in the late 1960s. They were distinctive because of their hoods, which featured a vertically corrugated design seen on the Norfolk & Western car on page 52. They had a 49'-4" inside length.

Whitehead & Kales, which was better known as a manufacturer of auto racks for flatcars, built 200 coil cars for DT&I in 1967 and 1968 (following a single experimental car, no. 1000, in 1965). The 263K GRL cars had fishbelly sideframes like the early Evans car, but had seven sets of paired vertical fastener heads spaced evenly along the side. Their hoods were unique: they were rounded, but had several widely spaced corrugations.

Modern coil cars

The move to 110-ton (286K GRL) cars in the 1990s led to higher-capacity coil cars. Trough length became standardized at 42 feet, although the exterior length of various manufacturers' cars varies by design.

Among the first 286K cars was Thrall's CoilShield, built for Conrail in anticipation of the increased weight standard in 1992. It's built as a well car, with the trough depressed between the trucks to give it a stable, low center of gravity. It has a one-piece cover with angled top, vertical external posts, and angled braces on each end panel. Conrail acquired 750 through 1995.

Johnstown America (now FreightCar America) has a 110-ton

Coil cars from National Steel Car have deep fishbelly side sills. This 110-ton car was built for Illinois & Missouri Rail Link in 2000. *Jeff Wilson*

Thrall's 110-ton car has channel-style side sills with a slight fishbelly drop between the trucks. Trinity continued building this design after acquiring Thrall in 2001. This one was built for Union Pacific in 1997. *Jeff Wilson*

Trinity built spine-style 110-ton coil cars for BNSF in 1998, named the Coil Care-XL. This one shows the heavy center sill with thin floor and insulated one-piece hood. *J. David Ingles*

coil car that has channel side sills with a slight step-down on the bottom edge. Vertical stiffeners are located along the sills. The cars have one-piece rounded covers, with a sharper curve angle than other builders' covers.

One of the most-common modern cars is the National Steel Car 110-ton design. It has distinctive deep fishbelly side sills and a single-piece insulated, rounded cover.

Trinity's 110-ton cars are based on the Thrall design (Trinity acquired Thrall in 2001). They have channel-style side sills with a slight step down along the bottom lip and single-piece

rounded covers.

Trinity also built several hundred spine-style coil cars for BNSF in 1997 and 1998, branded as Coil Care-XL cars. These cars have a heavy fishbelly center sill with just a thin body platform, giving them a distinctive appearance. They have single-piece rounded hoods.

Further information

James Kinkaid wrote an excellent article on the Evans coil cars in the October 1996 issue of *Mainline Modeler*, including a roster and drawings. David Casdorph offers a print-on-demand book, *The Coil Car Directory* (CreateSpace, 2011), which lists roster and builder information for the 19,000 cars built through 2011 (available through Amazon); *NSC Coil-Steel Freight Cars* (David Casdorph, 2012); and a Kindle book, *Coil Steel Freight Cars in Color* (2018).

CHAPTER SIX

LPG
(propane and butane)

Dual-diameter "whale belly" tank cars were common in the mid- to late 1960s. ACF built this 33,620-gallon, 100-ton car for its lease fleet in 1966. It's an ICC 112A 340W (non-insulated) car leased to Technical Propellants and carrying a load of LPG in 1969. It has older-style "DANGEROUS" placards.

J. David Ingles collection

Liquefied petroleum gas (LPG) has been used as a home fuel since the 1920s, and has since found many uses in industry as a feedstock for making plastics and other materials, as a fuel, and as a propellant. Railroads began carrying LPG at the beginnings of its popularity and still carry significant amounts, as LPG—unlike other petroleum products—doesn't travel by pipeline.

In the early 1900s, as more and more automobiles hit the roads, the primary goal of the growing oil refining industry was turning crude oil into as much gasoline as possible. The lightest gas fractions—methane and ethane (which make up natural gas) as well as butane and propane—were considered waste materials and burned off at the refinery.

By the 1920s, refineries began capturing and storing propane and butane. They could be compressed into liquid form at relatively low pressure (about 100 psi at 70 degrees F), making them practical to store in pressure vessels. Liquefied petroleum gas is a combination of butane and propane in varying ratios (depending upon the intended use), and the terms LPG, butane, and propane are sometimes used interchangeably. An odorant is also added to most LPG to make it easy to identify leaks.

By the 1930s, LPG began increasing in popularity as a home fuel, especially in rural areas, replacing coal and wood. The move was led in 1929 by Phillips, which sold it as "Philgas." LPG is different from the manufactured gas ("coal gas") that was used in major metropolitan areas and from the natural gas that would take over from coal gas after World War II, when pipelines were completed across many areas of the country. (See "LPG vs. natural gas" on page 61).

Distributors in small towns and cities began carrying LPG, with

American Car & Foundry built this car for Union Tank Line in 1931, making it one of the first LPG cars in service. The 11,000-gallon ICC 105 car is insulated, with the outer jacket slightly overlapping the end. *Union Tank Line*

This General American 11,000-gallon LPG car, built in 1947, is leased to Phillips Petroleum. Note the open ends of the bolsters compared to the ACF/Union car above. *TRAINS magazine collection*

The bonnet on a pressure car includes valves for the three loading/unloading connections (two product, one air) and the safety valve (cylinder in the center). This is in Oklahoma in 1939. *Russell Lee, Library of Congress*

This new 50-ton, 11,700-gallon LPG car was built by ACF in 1957 for Phillips. It's a non-insulated ICC 112A 400W car. Note the difference in ends compared to earlier insulated cars. It still has a center sill, but instead of straps the end anchors are welded to the tank. *ACF Industries*

many local fuel dealers expanding their gasoline and fuel oil businesses to include LPG. It was typical for railroads to deliver LPG to distributors and dealers by railcar, with trucks then delivering the product to final customers.

LPG was often called "bottle gas" for the portable tanks that could be picked up at (or delivered by) dealers. A common standard size was the 100-pound tank, which is 18" in diameter and four feet tall. Many rural and small-town homes soon had their own on-site tanks, typically 500 to 1,000 gallons, served by a bulk delivery truck.

Early pressure tank cars

LPG can't be carried in standard (non-pressure) tank cars, as it must be kept under pressure to keep it liquefied. Exposing LPG to the atmosphere releases the pressure and causes the liquid to boil, turning it to vapor.

The first high-pressure tank cars appeared in the late 1910s, initially for chlorine (see Chapter 2) and sulfur dioxide. The first car for LPG was built in 1928, a flatcar carrying multiple cylinders. By 1930, LPG tank cars were being built, to ICC specification 105. These cars became more common by 1940 and later as LPG continued growing in popularity as a fuel.

Pressure cars for LPG have welded heavy steel construction, providing for a test pressure of at least 300 psi. These

General American built this 14,600-gallon, ICC 112A 400W LPG car for Phillips in 1957. Note the differences in bolster and securing-strap design compared to the ACF car above. *General American*

General American built this multi-diameter (99" at ends, 118" in middle) 30,300-gallon, 70-ton LPG tank car in 1961. Leased to Phillips, it's on display at the GATX plant, posed next to an older 4,000-gallon tank car at right. *General American*

cars don't have manways with covers allowing access to the tank like a standard car (or large expansion domes like standard tank cars through the 1950s). Instead, the housing protects the loading and unloading pipe connections (two for product, one for air to control pressure), control valves, and a safety valve. There's no bottom

outlet on a pressure car like there is on a general-service non-pressure car.

Early LPG cars (and all ICC-105 cars) are insulated, with the tank wrapped with an insulating blanket, which is then covered by a thinner steel outer sheathing. The thermal insulation is not meant to insulate the contents but to provide protection in case the car is exposed to fire. From the late 1950s onward, many LPG cars have been built to ICC-112 specifications (later DOT-112), which are uninsulated. This is stenciled on the right end of each side, including the ICC or DOT number and test pressure.

Since LPG is relatively light (just 4.6 pounds per gallon compared to 6 pounds for gasoline and 7 pounds for diesel fuel), LPG cars could be proportionally larger than the typical 6,000- and 8,000-gallon cars of the period. Through the early 1940s LPG cars were typically 10,500-gallon cars; in the late 1940s this increased to 11,000 gallons.

Most early LPG cars were built by American Car & Foundry and General American. Both had exterior side sheathing extending slightly over the ends, creating a distinctive lip. General American's car was distinguished

MODELING TIP

LPG tank car models

Atlas has made HO and N scale models of early ACF 11,000-gallon LPG tank cars as well as a 1960s-prototype whale-belly car. Athearn Genesis has an HO and N scale model of a modern 33.9K tank car.

Since LPG is used across the country, these cars can be found in trains of virtually all lines. You can model a propane distributor or dealer, have cars delivered to an industry that uses it in some fashion, or simply model the cars passing through. Single-car shipments are still common, as are groups of cars. Be sure your model cars are properly placarded and stenciled.

A Tuloma Gas tank car, leased from UTLX, carries a load of LPG in 1964. Union built the single-diameter, 100-ton tank car in the early 1960s. It has a narrow-diameter tank compared to later cars. *J. David Ingles*

A new 38,500-gallon, 100-ton, frameless LPG tank car poses for the Union Tank company photographer in September 1960. It's one of three such cars leased to Atlantic Refining Co. *Union Tank Line*

By the time this ACF tank was built in 1973, the trend was to wide single-diameter tanks. This frameless 33,300-gallon, ICC 112A 400W tank wears a plain white scheme and is owned by Flamegas Leasing Co. *J. David Ingles*

LPG vs. natural gas

LPG and natural gas are not the same. Natural gas is mainly methane and ethane, is lighter than air, and has a lower energy value than LPG. Compressing natural gas to liquid form requires extremely high pressure or extremely low temperature (-260 degrees F), making it difficult and expensive to transport. Most natural gas is shipped by pipeline as a gas, with large distribution pipeline networks directly to homes and businesses in urban areas.

LPG is mainly propane and butane, is heavier than air, easily compresses to a liquid, and has more energy value than natural gas (which is why gas appliances require separate settings for LPG and natural gas). LPG is not shipped by pipeline, relying on railcars, trucks, and ships for distribution.

Older tank cars were required to be fitted with head shields by December 1979. This DOT 112A 400W car, built by Union in 1971, received separate external head shields in October 1978. *Railway Progress Institute*

by the style of bolster at the end compared to the ACF car. Cars of the era had separate frames (center sills), with the tank itself strapped in place (with the straps hidden by the exterior sheathing).

Modern pressure cars

Two radical changes to tank car evolution took place in the early 1960s. The first was the move toward frameless tank cars, begun by Union Tank Car in the late 1950s. Instead of a separate center sill, the end bolsters are welded directly to the tank itself, with the tank transmitting all train forces. This simplified construction and made cars lighter.

The second change was the move to 100-ton cars (263K GRL) in 1963. Tank car builders and customers were quick to see the efficiency of carrying as much product as possible on a single car. Because LPG is such a low-density product, pressure cars carrying it were among the first tank cars to see greatly expanded size.

The first were multi-diameter (also called dual-diameter) cars, sometimes referred to as "pregnant whales" or fishbelly tanks. These had tanks with a smaller diameter at each end above the trucks, broadening to a wider diameter between the trucks (the top of the tank remained straight, with the tank expansion at the sides and bottom of the car). The challenge for builders was making the tank as large as possible while staying within Plate C clearance standards.

The late 1960s saw a flurry of large cars (exceeding Plate C) for LPG and various chemicals, such as the 38,000-gallon UTLX car on page 60.

General American built this 33,600-gallon LPG car. It has end ladders and a flat surface indented into the jacketing on each side to maintain Plate C clearance. The DOT 105J 400W car is carrying non-odorized LPG (stenciling at far right of car) in 2018. *Cody Grivno*

However, in November 1970 the ICC capped tank car size at 34,500 gallons and 263K GRL. After that point, most LPG cars were single-diameter cars approaching that size.

Modern LPG cars are typically 65 feet long, with top/bottom shelf couplers required on new cars after January 1979 (and retrofitted to older cars by early 1982). Thermal protection was required for tank cars carrying flammable materials by December 1980. A common feature is a flat side in the middle of the tank jacketing on each side to keep the car within Plate C limits. For this reason, most newer LPG cars have ladders at the ends or on the ends of the sides, offset from the center.

Tank cars were required to be fitted with head shields by December 1979. These could be retrofitted externally, as was done on many cars (see page 61); many older cars were rebuilt with shields added directly to the end. Cars built after that date have head shields as part of the tank jacket or tank itself. The coupler and shield requirements were to minimize risks from punctures caused by couplers on neighboring cars in derailments.

Tank specifications were taken over by the Department of Transportation (DOT) as of 1967. Most modern LPG cars fall into DOT classes 105A300W, 105J300W, 105J400W, 112J340W, and 112J400 ("J" indicates jacketed thermal protection; "T" is sprayed-on exterior thermal coating; "W" is a fusion-welded tank).

Car ownership and lettering

Revenue-service tank cars are all privately owned. Railroads do own fleets of tank cars, but they are for company service, mainly carrying fuel and oil. Oil companies and distributors sometimes own their own cars; major companies with LPG cars have included Cities Service, Gulf, Phillips, Shell, and Warren (the largest early private fleet, with about 2,000 LPG cars by the early 1950s). Union Tank Car (UTLX) has always owned the largest lease fleet, followed closely by General American (GATX). Other builders with significant fleets include ACF (Shippers Car Line, SHPX) and in modern times Trinity and Greenbrier, as well. Although owner/lessee logos and lettering were common through the 1960s, most modern LPG cars are simply lettered for the leasing company.

Some LPG cars wear a 12"-wide orange horizontal band centered on the tank, a result of a Canadian regulation enacted in 1990 requiring that marking on pressure and hazardous-materials cars. The U.S. never adopted the rule, and the requirement was soon dropped in Canada, but many cars carried the

This DOT 112J 340W car was built by ARI, the car-building division of ACF. It has offset side ladders and is carrying non-odorized LPG on the BNSF in Minnesota in 2016. *Jeff Wilson*

This modern Trinity LPG car has side ladders offset to maintain Plate C clearance. It's carrying non-odorized LPG in 2018. *Cody Grivno*

Further information

A great resource on early tank cars is Edward Kaminski's *Tank Cars: American Car & Foundry Company, 1865 to 1955* (Signature Press); other good books are James Kinkaid's *Tank Car Color Guide,* volumes 1 (early cars with center sills) and 2 (modern stub-sill cars), both by Morning Sun). Ed Hawkins wrote a thorough article on ACF Type 27 10,500-gallon LPG tank cars in Volume 7 of *Railway Prototype Cyclopedia*, including a detailed roster.

bands for many years afterward.

Commodity stenciling is required for LPG, so "LIQUEFIED PETROLEUM GAS" lettering will be found on the right end of each side. Hazmat placards would be on each side and end of loaded cars. These would be the older white style with red "DANGEROUS" lettering until 1975 (see the Technical car on page 56); after that, they will be the modern type with product numbers. Cars carrying non-odorized LPG (required for some industrial uses) will also have stenciling to that effect.

CHAPTER SEVEN

Flour and sugar

Airslide covered hoppers revolutionized carrying flour, sugar, and other powdered and granulated products in bulk. This 2,600-cubic-foot car, built in 1961, is leased to U and I Sugar in this 1968 view. It has the open end-platform style of early cars.
J. David Ingles

Bulk food raw materials such as flour and sugar were being shipped in large quantities by the early 1900s. Large-scale bulk handling was difficult because the products were easily contaminated, so bags and sacks in boxcars were the standard shipping method. By the 1940s, manufacturers and shippers were working on better ways of hauling the products, leading to specialized covered hoppers.

Hundred-pound bags were the common method of shipping flour through the 1940s. This single-sheathed Rock Island 40-foot boxcar has just been loaded at the Pillsbury Mill in Minneapolis in 1939. *John Vachon, Library of Congress*

Flour milling had become a huge industry by the late 1800s, with large-scale milling centers well established in Minneapolis, Minn.; Buffalo, N.Y.; and other areas. Sugar refineries, likewise, had become larger, centered in sugar beet-growing areas of the Midwest and West.

By the early 1900s, commercial bakeries and food-processing companies were using more of these products. Unlike commodities such as coal and grain, which can be carried in bulk in open hoppers or boxcars, flour and sugar are easily contaminated. Bugs, rodents, and mold can easily infest unprotected products, and water—even moisture from humidity and condensation—can ruin shipments.

Thus the standard method of shipping was small containers that could be managed by one or two workers, either by hand or by use of a hand cart or dolly. Flour was historically handled in wooden barrels that held 196 pounds (a measurement

that became the industry standard through much of the 1900s). By 1910, this had largely shifted to sewn cloth sacks each holding 100 pounds. Paper sacks began appearing in the 1910s, with smaller sizes intended for retail

sale. Sugar, likewise, was typically transported in 100-pound sacks.

A great deal of these products traveled by rail, with many long-distance shipments to end users located across the continent. The standard

Flour sacks were easily damaged and contaminated, so cars had to be tightly sealed and free of protruding nails and wood splinters. The walls, floor, and door openings were lined with paper. *John Vachon, Library of Congress*

Domino bulk car

An early attempt to carry bulk food products is this American Sugar Refining Co. (Domino brand) car. The Pennsylvania Railroad in 1951 built it by rebuilding an old boxcar into a covered hopper, with roof hatches and three outlet bays. The 40-foot long, 2,060-cf creation was a one-of-a-kind car, and remained on the ASRX roster into the 1980s.

Domino's unique bulk car is shown in service in 1967.
J. David Ingles

The Buffalo Creek Railroad, jointly leased by Erie and Lehigh Valley, served Buffalo's (N.Y.) flour-milling district. Its fleet of boxcars had special lining to protect flour sacks; the stenciling left of the door reads "SPECIAL WEEVIL CONTROL CAR. DO NOT CONTAMINATE. RETURN EMPTY TO BUFFALO FOR FLOUR RELOADING." *J. David Ingles*

 **MODELING TIP**

Sugar and flour cars

Models of various Airslide and pressure-differential covered hoppers are available in all scales. Flour mills can be very modelable subjects for a layout, as can sugar refineries and commercial bakeries and other end users. Flour and sugar cars can appear in trains in all areas of the country; you can model the traffic without modeling the industries. You'll find more of these cars at and near milling and refining areas.

General American's 2,964-cf Trans-Flo covered hopper, built in 1948, was the predecessor to the Airslide car, and was built for flour service. This one carries a faded Nabisco logo (at left) in this 1961 view. *John Ingles, J. David Ingles collection*

40-foot, 50-ton boxcar was the most common car used through the steam era.

Flour and sugar sacks are easily damaged, so the main requirement for boxcars was that they be clean, free from leaks in the roof and walls, and not have any protruding nails or wood or metal shards or splinters that could tear a bag. Paper lining was applied to the car floor and walls before loading. Calculating the load was simple: for a 50-ton boxcar, 1,000 100-pound bags was a full load. The method was labor-intensive and time-consuming, both at the mill/refinery and for the end user (wholesaler or food processor), which then had to unload, store, and re-handle the sacks before using them.

Even with the development of specialized bulk covered hoppers, plenty of flour was still shipped in bags in boxcars into the 1960s, especially to smaller processors that didn't have pneumatic handling and storage systems.

Covered hoppers

Covered hoppers by the 1940s carried products like cement, lime, phosphate, and carbon black. Food products,

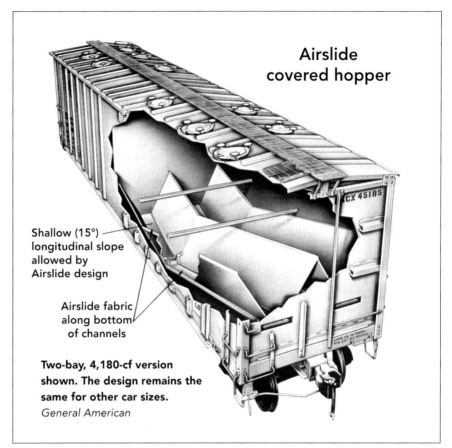

Airslide covered hopper

Shallow (15°) longitudinal slope allowed by Airslide design

Airslide fabric along bottom of channels

Two-bay, 4,180-cf version shown. The design remains the same for other car sizes. *General American*

General American's Airslide covered hopper, introduced in 1954, used air pressure through perforated fabric at the bottom of each bay to aerate powdered and granulated loads, effectively liquefying them for smooth unloading. *General American*

Through the 1960s, Airslide cars often carried the logos of their lessees, in this case Minnesota's Tennant & Hoyt, makers of Golden Loaf Flour. The 2,600-cf car, built in 1961, is shown in 1970. *J. David Ingles*

Brach's leased a variety of Airslide cars from General American, including this 4,180-cf car in sugar service. It was just a month old in this April 1974 photo. The larger two-bay cars lacked the end platforms of the smaller Airslides. *J. David Ingles*

Later 2,600-cf Airslides include an angled fillet at the top of each side at the end, giving them an appearance similar to a standard covered hopper. This former Rock Island car, built in 1968, was owned by Seaboard Allied Milling (a division of Cargill) by this 1982 scene. *J. David Ingles collection*

however, require stricter protection from contamination: better sealing roof and outlet hatches, a clean interior (either stainless steel or a coated lining to protect lading), and a method of pneumatically unloading products.

The first covered hopper specifically designed for flour was General American's Trans-Flo, built starting in 1948. The car was designed in conjunction with food company Nabisco and the Fuller Co., a Pennsylvania-based company that developed methods of air-driven pumping of powdered materials—mainly for the cement industry, but applicable to others as well.

The Trans-Flo had truss-style external bracing, two compartments with six paired outlet bays, and four pairs of round roof hatches. The 70-ton car measured 53 feet long and had stainless-steel compartments to protect food-grade products. It also had a Duryea double-cushion underframe. Although not many were built (about 60), General American applied what

ACF introduced its Pressureaide line of pressure-differential covered hoppers in 1979 with this 5,000-cf car. Air pressure applied to the interior forces the lading out for pneumatic unloading. The cars can be spotted by their external piping along the outlet bays. *ACF Industries*

Trinity built this 5,125-cf pressure-differential car in 1989. The 263K GRL car strongly resembles North American's earlier design, with rounded sides and angled, boxy ends. *Jeff Wilson*

it learned in developing its hugely successful Airslide cars.

The Trans-Flo required pneumatic unloading but did not apply internal air pressure. A car vibrator was used to free product that tended to stick to car walls and bays. Promotional materials touted that it took four hours for a single worker to unload a car.

Airslide cars

Further developments with the Fuller Co.—which General American acquired in 1954—led to a revised car design that would revolutionize carrying flour, sugar, and other powdered and granular materials: the Airslide covered hopper. They would soon become the most popular car for flour and sugar as well as many other products.

The key improvement over the Trans-Flo design was an outlet bay that used air pressure to aid unloading, eliminating the problem of product clumping and not flowing readily through the outlet. The diagram on page 67 shows the idea. The bottom angled portions of the outlet bays are lined with a heavy fabric (¼" thick), treated with silicone to make it slippery, and perforated with fine holes. During unloading, air at low pressure is forced through the fabric. This aerates the product, fluidizing it so it flows easily to the outlet. The Airslide

Trinity modified the design of its PD cars, revising the ends to more closely resemble conventional covered hoppers. This 5,660-cf, 110-ton car was built in 2006 and leased to North Dakota Mill & Elevator, the country's largest flour mill as of 2022. *Cody Grivno*

The National Sugar Refining Co. had a fleet of non-pressure covered hoppers for carrying sugar. This 2,442-cf car is lined and insulated and has tight-fitting roof hatches and gravity-pneumatic outlets. *TRAINS magazine collection*

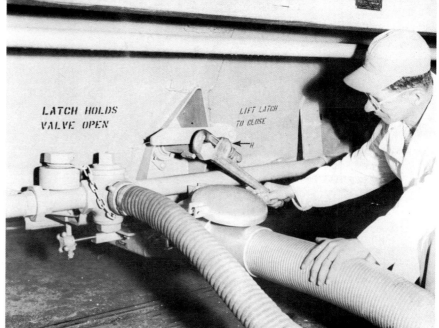

A worker positions the flour loading hose above a hatch on a pressure-differential covered hopper. *CSX*

To unload an Airslide car, a 3" hose is connected to an external air source (left). The large hose at right pneumatically unloads the car. Pressure-differential cars work in similar fashion. *General American*

fabric allows a very shallow angle of the longitudinal bays, increasing the interior capacity of the car.

Externally, Airslide cars are distinctive compared to other covered hoppers. The initial cars were single-bay, 2,600-cubic foot cars, and they were the primary type built into the early 1960s. They had open end platforms with framework and were available as 50- or 70-ton cars. In 1965, the end design was changed slightly to include an angled fillet at the top, making them look more like a conventional covered hopper.

The car was soon offered in a 3,600-cf, two-bay version. The design resembled the smaller car; longer, but still with braced end platforms. Another longer version appeared in the

1960s: 4,180 cubic feet. On these cars the side panels extended to the ends, eliminating the end platforms. They have a distinctive boxy appearance. These cars were 70- or 100-ton capacity.

General American continued building Airslides into the early 1980s; it ceased building railcars in 1984. By that time, the trend was moving toward pressure-differential cars. Many Airslides remained in service into the 2000s, but they are rare in the 2020s.

By the 1970s, a fairly common practice was to join two 2,600-cf Airslides together with a drawbar and treat the pair as a single car. This gave the shipper and consignee the advantage of a larger car while the railroad handled it as a single car shipment.

Flour- and sugar-service Airslide cars were often leased by shippers, and many wore the logos of their lessees. Many railroad-owned cars were also in flour and sugar service, and would be stenciled to that effect.

Pressure-differential cars

A variation on the Airslide is the pressure-differential car. These cars resemble conventional covered hoppers, but with additional piping along the outlet bays. During unloading, the interior compartment is pressurized, forcing lading out of piping attached to the outlet gates. They are commonly used for flour, sugar, and other fine materials prone to clumping.

The first of these, built by ACF in 1964 for New York Central, were

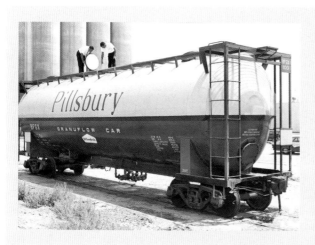

Granuflow covered hopper

The Granuflow car was built by Richmond Tank Car to a B.F. Goodrich design. It had a tank body (but was still classified as a covered hopper) and used air and a perforated urethane foam lining at the bottom (called the "Granu-Flor") to liquefy the lading. It also had an inflatable lining on the lower side walls (the "Granu-Flator") to prevent the load from sticking to the walls. Only three of the 3,000-cf capacity cars were built: the one shown, owned by Goodrich and lettered for Pillsbury; and two for Santa Fe.

The Granuflow was an experimental tank-style covered hopper developed by Goodrich and built in 1963 by Richmond Tank car. *B.F. Goodrich*

Flour is being transloaded from a Chessie System covered hopper to a bulk highway trailer via a truck-mounted pump for final delivery to a commercial bakery in 1984. This is a common practice at team tracks. *Chessie System*

heavy (125-ton capacity) cars for cement (they were dubbed "Flexi-Flo" cars—see Chapter 4). In 1979 ACF branded the concept with its popular Center Flow design as the Pressureaide car. The cars can be spotted by the horizontal piping running alongside the outlet bays below the side sills (top pipe for air; bottom pipe for lading). Pressureaide cars have been built in a variety of sizes, including 3,300-, 5,000-, 5,300-, and 5,750-cf versions.

North American also built a line of pressure-differential covered hoppers from the late 1960s through 1985. They have curved-sided bodies with angled ends, with a recessed solid area at the end. Piping runs along the bottom outlet bays. The 100-ton cars were built in three sizes as the PD3000 (2,785 cf), PD4000 (3,900 cf), and PD5000 (5,150 cf). They were often used for flour and sugar as well as other products (see Chapter 4 on cement). Trinity and Thrall also built cars to a similar design.

Modern pressure-differential cars are typically 110-ton cars (286K GRL), and are built in multiple sizes for various ladings. In identifying cars, look at overall size, the shape of the body and ends, and the number and type of roof hatches and outlet bays.

Standard (non-pressure) covered

hoppers have also been used to carry flour and sugar. They will have tight-sealing roof hatches, interior lining for food products, and pneumatic outlets.

Loading and unloading

Regardless of the specific car type, flour and sugar require care in loading and unloading. Cars are loaded via roof hatches. Cars have individual hatches (as opposed to the long trough hatches used for grain). These hatches are made in various designs and are sealed tightly, with marking seals applied so that the receiver can tell if a hatch has been opened or tampered with.

Loading is done in a closed manner. The photo on page 70 shows how flour is loaded, with a loading pipe with a round plate that sits firmly over the hatch opening. This prevents contamination of the load by any outside particulates, and also limits dust created by the loading process.

Unloading is done pneumatically. Most commercial bakeries and food processors were converting their facilities to bulk handling for flour and sugar by the mid-1950s. While some used gravity-based systems (with screw-type augers), the merits of air-based systems (and the lower risk of product contamination) made

Further information

The January 1987 issue of *Mainline Modeler* includes a roster of all railroads and private owners who bought or leased Airslide cars, with the number operated and car capacity. *Freight Cars Journal Monograph no. 26*, by David Casdorph, provides a good history of pressure-differential cars.

The Model Railroader's Guide to Industries Along the Tracks: 3, by Jeff Wilson (Kalmbach, 2008) has a chapter on sugar beet refineries and operations. *The Model Railroader's Guide to Grain*, by Jeff Wilson (Kalmbach, 2015), includes a chapter on mills and milling, plus the freight cars used.

pneumatic systems most common.

A hose is connected to the outlet gate for the product. For Airslide and PD cars, another hose is connected to the car's air inlet pipe. Unloading can be directly into a storage tank at a factory or processor; transloading to trucks for final delivery is also quite common, done either at a railroad team track or a private transloading center. In this case, the truck's air system can be used or a portable pump can move the product.

CHAPTER EIGHT

Coal

**The USRA two-bay, 50-ton hopper
was the first common coal car design
built in large numbers. This Colorado
& Southern (Chicago, Burlington &
Quincy subsidiary) car, built in 1919
and here carrying a coal load in 1959,
has been rebuilt with a 55-ton capacity
and new AB brakes (the brake lever
on the end replaced the original
horizontal brake wheel).**
J. David Ingles

Although rail coal traffic is down significantly since peaking

at 7.7 million carloads in 2008, U.S. railroads still carried 3.3

million carloads in 2021. This makes coal the most common

commodity on the rails, accounting for 27 percent of total

rail tonnage originated.

This Andersons hopper car, shown in 1961, is a former Wabash panel-side rebuild of a USRA two-bay car. The panels expanded the capacity to 2,120 cf. *John Ingles, J. David Ingles collection*

Toledo, Peoria & Western No. 4035 is a non-AAR standard two-bay offset-side 50-ton car, with seven evenly spaced stamped ("hat-shaped") stiffeners along the side. The rivet lines follow the interior posts and slope sheets. *Montague L. Powell, J. David Ingles collection*

Railroads have always carried a lot of coal, and coal operations and cars have changed significantly through the years. Into the 1940s the railroads themselves were major coal customers, as steam locomotives burned significant amounts of the fuel. A great deal of single-car shipments of coal went to local dealers for resale to homes and businesses, as coal was a primary fuel for home heating (more than 100 million tons per year at its peak), and coal dealers were common in small towns and large cities alike.

That changed significantly from the 1950s onward as steam locomotives were retired and coal gave way to natural gas, LPG, and fuel oil for home heat. Today, 90 percent of coal goes to power plants, with much of the rest used in steel production. Most of this now travels in unit trains, with 70 percent of coal coming from five states (Wyoming, West Virginia, Pennsylvania, Illinois, and Kentucky).

Mining has also changed. Through the 1950s there were hundreds of mines, many of which loaded out just a few cars a day. Those disappeared through the 1970s, and today, huge mines load out trainloads each day.

Coal cars

Starting in the late 1800s, the term "coal car" became synonymous with the bottom-dump hopper car. Hoppers were among the first steel cars in the 1890s due to the beating they took in service. They have floors that slant downward to two, three, or more sets of angled outlet doors in bays below the floor.

Coke service cars

Coke is coal that has been heated in an air-free environment, which drives off impurities and concentrates the carbon content, resulting in a gray-appearing rock higher in energy content than coal. It's mainly used as an ingredient in steel making. Railroads move coke in much smaller quantities than coal, and since coke is lighter than coal, some railroads have specialized cars for hauling it. This can be done by extending the sides of conventional hopper cars or building new cars with higher cubic capacity. These cars are usually prominently labeled "FOR COKE SERVICE ONLY," as accidentally loading them with coal would put them significantly over their weight limits.

Norfolk & Western no. 76435 is an Ortner Rapid Discharge hopper built in 1965 specifically for carrying coke (stenciling at left reads "FOR COKE LOADING ONLY." At 5,390 cf, it dwarfs the 2,460-cf coal hopper to the right of it, even though both are rated at 70 tons. *John Ingles, J. David Ingles collection*

This Monon car is an AAR twin-bay, 55-ton, offset-side design, with nine angle-style stiffeners spaced unevenly. It was built in 1954 and has a 2,145-cf capacity. Note the difference in the beveled angles of the end panels compared to the TP&W car on page 73. *TRAINS magazine collection*

Hopper cars are typically identified by their number of bays, their estimated capacity in tons, and by their capacity in cubic feet. They are further identified by their basic body construction: outside braced (exterior post) or offset-side, with smooth exteriors over inside posts.

Gondolas have also been used to carry coal since the early 1900s. Larger gondolas became more common in the 1960s and later as many power plants began receiving unit trains of gondolas equipped with rotary couplers, using rotary dumpers to empty them.

The huge amount of coal traffic through the years means that the

The AAR three-bay, 70-ton, offset-side hopper was a common coal carrier from the 1940s into the 1960s. This Chicago, Burlington & Quincy car was built in 1951 and rebuilt and repainted in 1962. *John Ingles, J. David Ingles collection*

MODELING TIP

Coal car operations

If you model any period into the 1950s, you can have single two- and three-bay hopper cars (or strings of cars) mixed into trains on their way to local coal dealers and small industries, and in coal territory, having various car types running as complete trains. Modeling coal loads of different lump sizes will make models stand out.

Single-car traffic dropped off considerably in the 1960s. After that point, the emphasis is on unit trains or movements of large cuts of cars traveling from mines to power plants and steel mills. These traveled from mines to utilities across the country, so many main and secondary lines hosted unit trains.

The Norfolk & Western built 13,500 cars to its H2a design from 1948-1956. it is a 70-ton, three-bay, 2,460-cf car with eight vertical side posts and angled end heap shields. This car was built in 1948 and is shown in 1958. *John B. Corns collection*

number of different coal-car designs built is staggering. There have been ARA and AAR standards for cars, and many manufacturers and individual railroads built cars to their own designs. It's impossible to cover all of the variations that have been used. We'll take a look at the most common cars, but if you model a specific railroad that handles a lot of coal traffic, look to articles, websites, and books for more information.

Steam-era hopper cars

One of the first common hopper car designs was the United States Railroad Administration (USRA) 50-ton, two-bay car. It was one of the standard car designs developed during USRA control of U.S. railroads during World War I. A total of 22,000 were built during USRA control, with another 29,000 clones or similar cars built through the 1920s.

The USRA car was 30 feet long and 10'-8" tall with a 1,880-cf capacity. It was an exterior-post car with seven vertical posts and a vertical brake staff at the B end. Many survived in service through the 1950s. They were often

General-service (GS) 42-foot gondolas were often used to haul coal through the steam era. This 50-ton composite-side car was built by American Car & Foundry for Louisville & Nashville in 1919. *TRAINS magazine collection*

Virginian's six-axle, 105-ton "battleship" coal gondolas were the largest freight cars in regular service in the early 1900s. Number 19611 was built in 1920 and is at Victoria, Va., in the 1940s. *TRAINS magazine collection*

Norfolk & Western No. 100054 is a class GKd 90-ton coal gondola built in 1927. It rides on six-wheel trucks and has angled heap shields atop each end. *Norfolk & Western*

Southern's 100-ton aluminum "silversides" cars were the first modern coal gondolas. Compare No. 1111's size to that of the hopper car to which it's coupled at right. Pullman-Standard built the 52-foot, 3,620-cf cars in 1960; this view is from 1963. *J. David Ingles collection*

rebuilt, and one common modification was to add extension panels between the posts on each side. Rebuilds also received upgraded brakes (AB replacing the original K brakes, with modern geared brake wheels) and upgraded trucks, which could boost the weight limit to 55 tons.

The USRA also published a design for a 70-ton, three-bay car, and although none were built during USRA control, 21,000 were built in the 1920s. The height remained the same, but the length was stretched to 40'-5" for a 2,508-cf capacity. They were distinctive in that the middle bay had twin discharge doors set at a much higher level than the end bays.

A new style of car with smooth exterior sides appeared starting in 1924. Known as offset-side cars (for the side being offset to the exterior of the posts), these cars had sides angled inward at the top, with multiple triangular stiffeners matching the locations of the vertical posts along the top. The first two-bay cars had seven evenly spaced stiffeners and were known as the Enterprise design (for the Enterprise Railway Equipment Co.). More than 12,000 were built through the 1940s by many builders as well as railroad shops.

The most common coal car of the 1930s to 1950s was the Association of American Railroads (AAR) offset-side

The first coal cars with rotary couplers for unit-train service were these 100-ton, 4,000-cf gondolas built by Thrall for Commonwealth Edison in 1964. Thrall would build many cars to this basic design, with angled sides, ends, and posts. *John Ingles, J. David Ingles collection*

Thrall's later design had vertical sides and posts. This aluminum version was built as a 100-ton car in 1990 for Detroit Edison and converted to 110-ton capacity (286K GRL) a few years later. It's shown in 2006. *Jeff Wilson*

50-ton car, adopted as a standard in 1934. The AAR design had nine angle stiffeners across the top of each side, spaced unevenly (matching the interior post locations). The first cars were 32 feet long; in 1946, the design was revised by making it two feet longer, increasing the capacity to 55 tons (most were 2,145 cf). About 127,000 were built through the mid-1950s.

The cars had many detail variations. The stiffeners were stamped metal (often called "hat-shaped") on early cars; those on later cars were usually steel angles. Stiffener spacing also varied. Some cars were built to a shorter height, and these generally had stiffeners with more even spacing. Brakes, trucks, and other appliances also varied among cars.

A 70-ton offset-side car first appeared in the late 1920s: a four-bay, 40-foot car. About 14,000 were built through 1930. The 70-ton design was then redesigned, becoming a three-bay, 41-foot car with a 2,773-cf capacity (the design was stretched by 12" in 1946). This proved more popular, with about 32,000 built through the 1950s.

Along with these cars, many exterior-post cars were built in various two- and three-bay designs by several manufacturers and railroads—namely coal-haulers such as Norfolk & Western, Virginian, and Chesapeake & Ohio. Spotting features include the car dimensions (height and length), number of posts, side-sill design, cubic-foot capacity, and shape of the ends (slope sheets, end panels, and bracing). Many of these cars have vertical extensions at the ends ("heap shields") to allow them to be more fully loaded.

By the late 1950s, as car weight

Greenville's coal gondolas had alternating heavy and light posts along each side. This 100-ton, 3,700-cf car is in Greenville's leasing fleet in 1966; it carries Consolidated Coal Co.'s logo and lettering. *John Ingles, J. David Ingles collection*

limits increased, railroads were moving from deliveries to small coal dealers (which often preferred the smaller cars) to larger industrial and power plant customers. For these, as well as deliveries to lake and ocean ports, railroads wanted the largest cars possible.

Early gondolas

Some railroads in the steam era preferred gondolas for carrying coal.

The Santa Fe, Rio Grande, Milwaukee Road, and many others used large numbers of GS (general-service) drop-bottom gondolas for coal traffic; many railroads used both hoppers and gondolas based on customers' preferences.

In the 1910s, some eastern railroads, notably Chesapeake & Ohio, Norfolk & Western, and Virginian, built high-capacity (90- to 105-ton) gondolas—often called "battleship"

gons—to move coal from mines to ports where rotary dumpers unloaded coal for transfer to ships.

These cars were notably huge in a period where 40- and 50-ton cars were standard. They had tall sides, rode on six-wheel trucks, and were equipped with dual brake systems to handle their heavy weight. With few exceptions, they were restricted to on-line use shuttling coal to ports; this type of car would not be found traveling cross

The most popular coal gon of the 1980s to the 2000s is the BethGon Coalporter, marked by slope-sheet ends and rounded tubs between the trucks. This 110-ton, 4,437-cf aluminum version was built by Johnstown America in 1997. *Jeff Wilson*

The ACF Coalveyor is a 100-ton car that resembles the older Greenville design, but with a different side sill and a below-floor extension. This 4,040-cf car is serving Dairyland Power Cooperative in 1995. *J. David Ingles*

country making deliveries to local coal dealers.

The Virginian's 2,025 cars were the largest, with a 105-ton capacity. They were 50 feet long and 11'-1" tall, with offset sides and a 3,840-cf capacity. Empty, each weighed about 74,000 pounds; compare this to a modern 110-ton aluminum coal gon, which weighs about 46,000 pounds.

The C&O's 1,000 cars resembled the Virginian's, having offset sides, but

were shorter (44 feet) and carried 90 tons of coal with a 3,212-cf capacity. Norfolk & Western's 1,750 cars were built to several designs from 1912 to the early 1920s. They were 45 feet long, 10'-4" tall, and carried 90 tons of coal, with a light weight about 65,000 pounds. Most of these big cars remained in service for 30 to 40 years and were retired in the late 1950s.

Another railroad noted for early coal gondolas was Chicago & Illinois

Midland, which used 70-ton gondolas built in the 1940s to carry coal for Commonwealth Edison. The C&IM's 500 cars were 48 feet long and 9 feet tall, with a 2,778-cf capacity.

Unit trains and modern coal gondolas

The coming of unit trains for coal traffic in the early 1960s led to larger cars and the emergence of the modern coal gondola and hopper, with advances

The Aeroflo is a lightweight car from Johnstown America. The aluminum car has interior posts with vertical seams on the sides. This car was built for Burlington Northern in 1994 and is carrying coal on BNSF in the early 2000s. *Jeff Wilson*

including roller-bearing trucks, lightweight construction, and rotary couplers.

A unit train is more than a solid train of coal cars; it's a complete train loaded at one mine and delivered to a single customer on a single waybill. The first unit coal trains of the 1960s were typically at least 75 cars, and today's unit trains are usually 100 to 125 cars. Unit trains commonly (but not always) are made up of cars of the same type, and have the same owner—either the utility company or the railroad that originates or delivers the load.

Many utilities choose to buy or lease their own cars to keep them in dedicated service, while others rely on cars supplied by railroads. Coal deliveries are scheduled by need, with contracts negotiated by the coal provider and railroads. The popularity of unit trains grew in the 1970s and later, and although some coal is still handled in smaller lots, the majority is destined to generating plants via unit trains.

The first modern 100-ton (251K GRL) coal gondolas were also revolutionary for their aluminum construction. Southern's 750 cars, built by Pullman-Standard in 1960,

were dubbed "silversides" for their appearance. They were 52 feet long with a 3,620-cf capacity.

The first coal gons with rotary couplers were 270 cars with 4,000-cf capacity built by Thrall for Commonwealth Edison in 1964. The end with the rotary coupler was painted a contrasting color, a practice that continues today. Thrall continued building similar cars in varying capacities, and they featured heavy vertical exterior posts with slides that tapered slightly inward at the bottom. Thrall's later 100- and 110-ton cars had thinner posts and vertical sides.

Early rotary dumpers required cars to be switched into position one at a time. The early 1960s saw the introduction of rotary dumpers that could, with the use of rotary couplers, allow trains to be unloaded without uncoupling—a major time-saver. Most large utilities quickly added these dumpers, and by the 1970s most unit-train coal cars had rotary couplers. The dumpers required cars of a specific length: 53'-1", with a coupled length of 53'-7". Car capacity varies from about 3,700 to 4,100 cubic feet.

Other manufacturers were soon building coal gondolas. Greenville's

design resembled Thrall's, but had alternating heavy and light posts along each side. Pullman-Standard's cars had lighter vertical posts with car sides that were vertical, with non-terminating ends (horizontal corrugations, with the car sides extending over the ends of the corrugations).

To increase car capacity without increasing length, the "bathtub" design was introduced. These cars feature a long tub that extends below normal floor level between the trucks. Canadian Pacific was the first to get them, in 1969. Built by Hawker Siddeley, the cars were five feet longer than standard rotary service cars (4,760 cf) and did not have rotary couplers.

The most popular bathtub car has been the BethGon Coalporter, first built by Bethlehem in 1978 and continued by successors Johnstown America and FreightCar America (as the BethGon II). The car has hopper-style slope-sheet ends, vertical posts, and rounded tubs below floor level. They have been built in steel, aluminum (which became popular for coal cars in the 1980s), and hybrid versions in varying capacities: 100- and later 110-ton cars from 4,000 to 4,911 cf.

Norfolk & Western's class H11 series of three-bay, 100-ton hoppers is among the most common modern hopper designs. Originally built in the 1960s, this Norfolk Southern H11CR car was rebuilt with a new body in 1992. *Jim Hediger*

Coal grades and sizes

All coal is not alike. Especially through the steam era, anthracite and bituminous coal were crushed and screened into sizes based on intended use. Bituminous—the most common type—ranged from slack (¾" and under) to stoker (up to 1¼"), nut (up to 2"), egg (to 5"), lump (5"), and mine run (5"-8"). Anthracite, or hard coal, was called buckwheat (⁹⁄₁₆" and under), pea (to ¹³⁄₁₆"), nut (to 1⅝"), stove (to 2⁷⁄₁₆") egg (to 3¼") and broken (to 6").

By the 1960s, the anthracite market had largely gone away, and most bituminous and sub-bituminous coal was uniform size, heading for large utilities.

In 1955, a small mine on the Louisville & Nashville is loading a two-bay AAR offset-side car with mine run coal at left (likely destined for a blast furnace) while a USRA two-bay car at right gets a load of egg coal (likely bound for a local coal dealer). *William A. Akin*

ACF offered a bathtub-style car that had sides resembling the old Greenville design. Called the Coalveyor, the 100-ton cars were built from 1978 through 1981. Union Pacific built similar 100-ton cars, but with side posts in a 1-2-1 (heavy/light/heavy) pattern and heavy V-bracing on the ends.

Trinity's original bathtub car,

the 110-ton Aluminator, strongly resembles the BethGon, but with tapered tubs (deeper at the ends and shallower at the middle). Trinity then shifted to a design with straight tubs very similar to the BethGon, but with a different end sill design.

Johnstown America in 1989 began building the Aeroflo, a lightweight (42,000-pound) smooth-side aluminum

car with prominent vertical seams. Early cars had solid end panels; later versions are open below the slope sheets.

Modern hopper cars

By 1960, construction was moving toward larger (100-ton) cars, with exterior-post designs becoming standard; the last offset-side car was built in 1960. Railroads—many of

Pullman-Standard built a lot of 100-ton rotary-coupler unit-train hoppers in multiple sizes in the 1970s. This Chicago & North Western 4,000-cf car was built in 1975. The end panel on the rotary (left) end is slightly wider than the brake (B) end at right (note how the wheel at right sticks out past the car end). *TRAINS magazine collection*

Bethlehem built this four-bay, 100-ton steel hopper for Missouri Pacific in 1980. The 3,715-cf car is shown in 1984.
J. David Ingles

This 110-ton (286K GRL) steel three-bay hopper was built for BNSF by FreightCar America in 2007. It has a 3,957-cf capacity and a rotary coupler (at right). It's in a BNSF train at Dassel, Minn., in 2016. *Jeff Wilson*

Quick-discharge hoppers have five outlet bays, with air-activated outlet gates on each side of each bay. This is a 4,300-cf Johnstown America AutoFlood car. *Jeff Wilson*

which built their own cars—and manufacturers all had their own ideas over what worked best, resulting in a wide range of designs.

To identify and differentiate cars, look at construction (aluminum or steel, welded or riveted); overall height and length; cubic capacity; whether it has rotary couplers, in which case it should follow the standard length for rotary cars; the number and style of bays and outlet doors; the number, spacing and style of side posts; and the style of the end platform and bracing. Most standard cars have three or four bays, with capacities ranging from 3,600 cf to 4,200 cf. Major builders have been Bethlehem (later Johnstown America and FreightCar America), Pullman-Standard, and Trinity.

A distinctive car pioneered by Ortner was the Rapid Discharge design. These cars have five or six outlet bays, with gates on either side of each bay, enabling the cars to unload much faster than a standard hopper car. Ortner was acquired by Trinity in 1984, and Trinity continued to offer upgrades of the design. Similar cars were later offered by other builders as well (Johnstown America's was the AutoFlood).

Weight-limit increase; traffic drop

Car construction moved exclusively to 110-ton (286K GRL) gondolas and hoppers by 1995, and many earlier 100-ton cars had been built to be easily converted (which was usually a matter of adding new trucks or upgrading the spring packages in older trucks).

The dramatic drop in coal traffic over the past decade has left railroads and utilities with an excess of cars. Many older coal gons have been scrapped or now serve as large mill gondolas in scrap-metal service. Orders for new coal-service cars have slowed considerably. The cars built from the 1990s through the 2010s will remain in service for a long time.

Further information

See *The Model Railroader's Guide to Coal Railroading* by Tony Koester (Kalmbach, 2006) for an in-depth look at the coal industry. It describes mines of various types, coal railroad operations, coal dealers, and various rail and mining equipment. The book *Coal Cars: The First Three Hundred Years* by Martin Robert Karig III (University of Scranton Press, 2007), provides an extensive summary of coal hoppers and gondolas, with lots of photos and illustrations.

CHAPTER NINE

Auto parts

The 86-foot excess-height auto-parts car was developed by railroads working with auto makers and freight-car builders. Pullman-Standard built this four-door (double doors on each side) car for Southern Ry. in 1966. The PS cars can be spotted by their proprietary ends and by the bottoms of the side posts visible along the side sill.

John Ingles, J. David Ingles collection

Railroads' extensive involvement in carrying finished autos has long been apparent in the strings of auto rack cars seen in trains across the country. What isn't always apparent is the huge business in bringing auto parts to assembly plants. Although railroads today don't carry the amount of parts traffic they once did, auto parts have historically been a key lucrative traffic source, requiring dedicated cars and expedited service.

Modern vehicles are made from 40,000 or more individual parts. Although some assembly plants make some components on site, most parts come in from outside factories and vendors, often from significant distances. Most auto makers have multiple assembly plants across the U.S. (as well as Canada and Mexico) specializing in specific models. Auto makers supply many of their own parts; one stamping plant may produce body panels for multiple assembly plants. Third-party companies produce everything from tires to batteries to castings to electronic modules to glass. All have varying sizes and weights and require care in shipping.

Since most parts travel in enclosed cars, how can we capture the essence of the traffic on model railroads? For starters, by choosing appropriate cars for the era being modeled. We can then give these cars the lettering, stenciling, and other details that give

A Pennsylvania Railroad auto parts train rolls along a main line in 1959. The 50-foot double-door cars are stenciled with their code/pool numbers showing their specific plant and product assignments. *J. David Ingles collection*

This ex-Pere Marquette (now Chesapeake & Ohio) double-door boxcar, built in 1946, is still in auto parts service in 1963. It is weathered, and repaint patches show that its code stenciling has changed over the years. The car also includes route stenciling on the door: "RETURN EMPTY TO C&O RY DETROIT MICH." *J. David Ingles collection*

clues about their contents. A huge part of this is operation. Auto parts often travel in blocks of cars (or sometimes entire trains), and these are on tight schedules receiving priority treatment, as a delayed car could result in an assembly line shutdown.

Early parts boxcars

Into the 1930s, auto parts were typically carried in standard boxcars. As parts traffic (and revenues from carrying it) increased as the Depression began easing and auto production stepped up in the late 1930s, railroads began equipping cars specifically for auto parts service—a practice that increased greatly in postwar years.

The AAR classified boxcars designed for parts as XAP (X for boxcar, A for auto, P for cars with specific fittings or racks to carry parts). Railroads and manufacturers equipped cars to carry specific parts and components, often building customized racks to carry them efficiently.

This led to railroads and manufacturers developing pools or

Into the early 1960s, many auto-parts boxcars had built-in internal racks for carrying specific components. This is a Pennsylvania Railroad class X29 car with steel racks. *Pennsylvania Railroad*

This Pennsylvania double-door boxcar, built in 1963, is one of 58 in its series equipped with racks for carrying auto transmissions from Ford's Sharonville (Cincinnati) plant. Its pool number (167) is above the reporting marks, with "RETURN WHEN EMPTY TO PRR CINCINNATI, OHIO" stenciling. *John Ingles, J. David Ingles collection*

MODELING TIPS

Modeling auto parts cars

Several model manufacturers have offered cars suitable for parts service. Look for opportunities to customize them. Decals and dry transfer lettering can be used for pool or code numbers or "RETURN TO …" stenciling. Check Shapeways. com for vendors offering kits for auto frame loads and other details.

Although auto assembly plants are beyond the scope of most model railroads, modeling a parts manufacturing plant can be done on a smaller scale. Look for scenes to model, such as parts racks or a car being loaded or unloaded.

A new Pullman-Standard boxcar equipped with Hydroframe-60 cushioning is spotted for unloading inside a building at Ford's St. Paul, Minn., assembly plant in 1960. *James Kinkaid collection*

This Pullman-Standard double-plug-door car, built for Louisville & Nashville in September 1963, is one of the first new-design 60-foot parts cars to enter service. It has welded exterior-post sides, fishbelly side sills, and roller-bearing trucks. *John Ingles, J. David Ingles collection*

groups of cars for specific types of parts (and serving specific plants). For example, if a group of 50-foot boxcars was needed to haul transmissions from Cincinnati to Detroit on a route that traversed three railroads, each railroad would contribute the percentage of cars that reflected their haul.

By the 1950s, this was reflected in markings on the cars. Along with the XAP stencil (next to the capacity figure), a one- to three-digit number or letter code located adjacent to the car's reporting marks and car number indicated the car's pool assignment. Additional stenciling would list the specific location to which empty cars should be returned. Since cars ran in pools, this might indicate an offline location on a railroad other than the car owner.

The majority of parts cars were 50-foot, 50-ton, double-door AAR boxcars, although some single-door and 40-foot cars were also used. Thousands of cars were needed for parts service, and their assignments (and often specific parts they carried) were listed in *Official Railway Equipment Registers.*

This system worked, but not efficiently. The specialized racks often needed to be modified and changed every model year, a huge expense,

and these cars couldn't be reassigned to other parts service without modification. Ups and downs in the market could idle cars, which—because of their equipment—couldn't be easily reassigned to other service.

Reassignments can be seen on older cars where old pool numbers and "RETURN TO …" stenciling have been painted out and new information added (see the Pere Marquette car on page 85).

By the late 1950s, the expense and

inefficiencies of managing parts cars— combined with larger trucks and the coming of Interstate highways—meant railroads were losing a lot of parts traffic to tractor-trailers.

Specialized 60-foot and 86-foot cars

The rebound in parts traffic began in 1961, when Ford approached the Wabash looking for new specialized high-capacity parts cars. Over the next three years, a cooperative effort

This 60-foot Chicago & Eastern Illinois parts car was built by Thrall in October 1963. It has smooth welded sides, shallow fishbelly side sills, double plug doors, and Dreadnaught ends. *John Ingles, J. David Ingles collection*

among the Big Three auto makers, 11 railroads, and several railcar manufacturers led to the adoption of two new basic boxcars: an excess-height 86-foot car for bulky, light-density parts (such as body stampings), and a 60-foot car for heavier components (such as transmissions and engine blocks).

The cars were designed to have a clear interior of a specific width and height. Instead of internal racks, parts would now be loaded into portable, reusable racks designed to fit the cars' dimensions. The racks could then be easily and quickly loaded at

their manufacturing plant aboard the boxcars, taken to the assembly plant, and transferred directly from the car to the assembly line. This meshed with auto makers' transition to "just-in-time" production to cut down on on-site parts inventory.

This also allowed cars to be easily transferred among assignments. While cars were still assigned to specific manufacturers and pools, the open interior design allowed them to be easily shifted to other pools as needed. This, and the cars' higher capacities compared to older 50-foot cars, allowed railroads to have fewer cars but

carry more traffic.

Although the new cars were built to common specifications, many variations still existed among manufacturers, including door sizes and styles (and width of openings), interior height, specific hardware, and side/end/roof design. All had cushioning devices, but they varied (end-of-car or underframe, length of cushion travel, and manufacturer). Most were built with roller-bearing trucks.

Major builders of 60-foot cars were ACF, Greenville, Pullman-Standard, and Thrall, and several railroads also

Greenville built this riveted-side, 60-foot double-plug-door parts car for Detroit, Toledo & Ironton in September 1963.
John Ingles, J. David Ingles collection

This 86-foot Santa Fe car was built by Thrall in May 1964. It includes lettering for "AUTO PARTS" as well as specific lettering for Ford, and is assigned to Ford's Buffalo, N.Y., stamping plant ("WHEN EMPTY RETURN TO WABASH RY. BUFFALO, N.Y."). The first of these big cars had running boards; this requirement was quickly eliminated. *John Ingles, J. David Ingles collection*

The riveted sides and recessed end panels and side sill mark this 86-footer as a Greenville-built car. It was delivered to Detroit, Toledo & Ironton in March 1970. *J. David Ingles*

built cars in their own shops. The first production cars began arriving in late 1963. Most were built to Plate C clearance, but some were slightly taller (to what eventually became Plate E); early cars had "exceeds Plate C" marking. Differences included side construction (exterior posts or smooth, welded or riveted), side sill style (straight, fishbelly, or channel), roofs (flat or peaked as well as pattern), door width, door style (single or double,

plug or sliding), and end style.

Pullman-Standard built many early cars with exterior posts; PS cars can also be spotted by the company's proprietary ends (heavy horizontal corrugations of uniform size) and roofs ("bow-tie" stamped design) and welded construction.

Greenville used riveted construction for side panels (with recessed end panels and side sill), while most other manufacturers used welded

construction. Thrall's cars typically had channel-style side sills. Other than PS, most manufacturers used Dreadnaught ends and diagonal-panel roofs.

Early cars had running boards, tall ladders, and high-mounted brake wheels. In 1966, running boards were eliminated on new cars, and ladders and brake wheels moved to a low position. Earlier cars were gradually modified.

By 1968, parts cars were being

Pacific Car & Foundry 86-foot cars featured external-post sides and deep center sills. This eight-door Southern Pacific car is open, showing a full load of racks marked "CHEV CLEVELAND." General Motors favored cars with two side-door openings. *Southern Pacific*

A forklift loads modular, stackable parts racks into a PC&F-built Southern Pacific 86-foot car assigned to General Motors. The portable racks greatly sped loading and unloading times compared to older cars with built-in racks. *Southern Pacific*

given the AAR designation XL or XML ("boxcar equipped with interior loading devices") instead of XAP, which covered other cars as well as auto parts cars. Code numbers were no longer common by the late 1970s, making it more difficult to identify cars in parts service (although "RETURN TO" stenciling was still common).

Many of these survived in auto parts service into the 2000s, but they have now been replaced by more modern cars.

High-cube cars

The big 86-foot cars were designed to push size limits as far as possible while still allowing travel along all major routes and matching clearance at plants' loading docks and buildings. The cars have an interior length of 86'-6" and are 94 feet long over the coupler faces. They have an interior height of 12'-9" and stand 17 feet tall, giving them a Plate E clearance.

Most were nominal 70-ton cars but some were 100-ton cars; a full load of stampings might only weigh 20 to 30 tons.

Greenville, Thrall, Pullman-Standard, and Pacific Car & Foundry built production cars (ACF and Whitehead & Kales each built single demonstration cars). More than 11,000 were eventually built. The first entered service in March 1964, and although the majority were built in the 1960s, some were built as late as 1978.

Greenville cars (4,800 built) had riveted construction, noticeable on the vertical side seams, with recessed lower side sills. The side panels behind the grab irons at the ends were recessed. The cars had Dreadnaught ends and diagonal-panel roofs.

Most Thrall cars (3,800) featured welded construction, but some had riveted side panels. Thrall cars had ladders at the ends of the sides instead of grab irons, and the cars had Dreadnaught ends and diagonal-panel roofs.

Pullman-Standard cars (2,400) were welded and had PS's distinctive proprietary ends (featuring heavy corrugations of uniform size) and roofs ("bow-tie" design).

PC&F built just an initial order of 200 cars (in 1964 for Santa Fe, St.

The new parts cars of the early 1960s featured smooth interior walls and floors. A rack of body stampings fits snugly into the end of an 86-foot car. *Southern Pacific*

Louis Southwestern, and Southern Pacific). They're easy to spot because of their distinctive outside-post construction.

Most 86-footers were four-door cars—a single 20-foot-wide opening on each side with a pair of 10-foot doors. General Motors, however,

specified eight-door cars (two 20-foot openings on each side) for cars serving its Chevrolet plants.

Initial orders of cars included running boards and full-height ladders (though no PS cars had them). The requirement was soon waived for these cars, and later cars had low-height

As older parts cars were retired from the 1990s onward, most remaining auto-parts traffic has traveled in 100- or 110-ton excess-height 60-foot boxcars. This 60-foot, 263K cushion-underframe car was built by Gunderson in 1997 for Norfolk Southern. *Jeff Wilson*

This Wabash auto-frame flat has a solid A frame on the B (left) end, with a tie-down bracket on the A end. It holds two rows of frames (84 total). The car was built in 1954 and assigned to pool 8A in this 1959 photo.
John Ingles, J. David Ingles collection

Several Pennsylvania Railroad gondolas are carrying loads of automobile frames in this late 1950s view. *Roderick H. Craib, Jr.*

By the late 1960s, frames were being carried in flat stacks aboard flatcars. Here several Trailer Train flats are carrying frames at Manassas, Va., in 1968. *J. David Ingles collection*

ladders and low-mounted brake wheels. Older cars were modified by having running boards removed and brake wheels moved by the early 1970s.

Most of these served into the 2000s, but were retired as they approached or hit 40 years old.

Further information

The book *Railroading & the Automobile Industry* by Jeff Wilson (Kalmbach, 2019) covers the history of the auto industry, along with the operations and cars involved (including auto racks and auto boxcars). Another great book with lots of photos and background information is *America's Driving Force: Modeling Railroads and the Auto Industry* (Wm. K. Walthers, 1998). If you model the 1940s to the 1960s, obtaining an *Official Railway Equipment Register* for the period you model will help you determine the cars in parts service at the time.

Traffic falloff, modern cars

The large fleets of 60- and 86-foot parts cars built in the 1960s and 1970s served well, with many lasting into the 2000s. Their numbers declined as they reached retirement age (40 years), matching a steep decline in auto parts traffic over recent decades. Railroads carried about 80 percent of auto parts traffic in 1970; by the 2020s, this dropped to less than 20 percent.

The auto parts traffic that remains is largely carried in standard 100-ton, excess-height 60-foot boxcars. Parts also travel via piggyback trailers and RoadRailer trailers.

Frame cars

One segment of parts traffic that is extremely visible is auto frames. Their bulk precludes moving them in boxcars, so historically they've travelled on modified gondolas and flatcars.

From the 1940s into the 1960s, frames were typically stacked on end at an angle—two rows of frames, side by side—against an A frame on one

end of a flatcar or gondola, with a tie-down bracket securing them at the other end and a floor rack to keep them aligned. The loading brackets had to be designed for specific frames. A disadvantage was that the frames had to be loaded and unloaded one at a time.

In 1963, at the request of Ford, several Trailer-Train member railroads worked to find a more-efficient method. The result was changing designs to allow the frames to be loaded flat, nesting with each other on brackets, in stacks. This allowed loading and unloading entire stacks of frames as one unit.

The first of these TTX frame flatcars—initially 60-footers—began appearing in 1964, with more than 500 in service by 1966. By 1970, 89-foot cars were being equipped, with 1,700 in service by 1977 and 3,200 in 2001. These cars can carry eight to 10 stacks of frames, with 10 to 14 frames per stack. About 1,500 remained in service as of 2020.

CHAPTER TEN

Frozen foods

Cryo-Trans No. 5064 is a modern 7,780-cf mechanical refrigerator car with an end-mounted refrigeration unit. The excess-height (Plate F) car, built by Gunderson in 2006, has a 72-foot inside length (82 feet overall) and smooth ends. *Jeff Wilson*

Frozen food traffic went from being almost nonexistent to a booming business within a 15-year span in the 1930s and 1940s. Railroads jumped in to carry this growing commodity, first with ice-bunker refrigerator cars, then with mechanical refrigerator cars designed specifically to handle frozen foods.

Santa Fe Refrigerator Dept. No. 5061 is a 50-foot steel ice-bunker refrigerator car with extra-heavy insulation for frozen-food service. It's one of 150 cars in its class built by General American for SFRD in 1940. Note the indentations behind the grab irons and ladder. *Santa Fe*

Although the concept of frozen foods as a method of preservation had been around for some time, the credit for creating the modern frozen-food industry goes to Clarence Birdseye. In the late 1920s, Birdseye developed machinery that could flash-freeze various foods. His company, Birds Eye, introduced the first popular line of frozen foods in 1930, which included

fish, vegetables, fruit, and meat.

The main challenge was getting these products from the manufacturing plant to warehouses and stores. Frozen foods require storage temperatures at or below 0 degrees F, and neither trucks nor railcars could provide this, especially for long-distance transport.

A boost that spurred development came in in the 1940s, when canned

goods were often in short supply due to the demands of the military during World War II. The frozen-food market grew, helped by more families acquiring electric refrigerators with frozen-food compartments and a growing number of stores selling frozen products.

Although sales dropped following the war, they began to pick up again by the early 1950s with the development

Western Fruit Express no. 70639 is a heavy-insulation ice-bunker car built by Pacific Car & Foundry in 1954. It's a 40-foot steel car with sliding plug door. The original reporting marks were "WHIX," but it lost its X by this early 1970s photo. *Jeff Wilson collection*

of products such as frozen french fries (1947), fish sticks (1952), and the big hit, TV dinners—which sold 10 million in 1954. A major product was frozen concentrated juice. Sales of this product soared from its first major push in 1945 (226,000 gallons produced) to 1954 (70 million gallons), most of it orange juice from Florida.

Ice-bunker cars

When the frozen-food market began growing in the 1930s, the only railroad technology available was the standard ice-bunker refrigerator car, used at that time for fresh fruits, vegetables, and meat—all of which required temperatures from the mid-30s to the 50s. Getting car temperatures well

below freezing presented a significant challenge.

Salt had long been used to obtain cooler temperatures, especially for meat cars. Salt causes ice to melt faster, resulting in colder temperatures. The amount of salt needed was significant for frozen foods, however—30% salt (typically a 10,000-pound load of ice with 3,000 pounds of salt), compared to 5% or 10% for other products. The cars also needed more frequent replenishment of both ice and salt because of the faster melting.

Even with that, the lowest temperature an ice-bunker car could generally achieve was about 5 degrees, and that was in ideal conditions. Car insulation of the period was quite inefficient—fiberglass and foam were still in the future—and summer temperatures made operations even more challenging. Short trips of one to three days were one thing, but a cross-country trip typically took 9 or 10 days. Precooling loads down to -10 degrees at the manufacturing plant helped, and cars were cooled with full ice/salt loads for 24 hours before loading.

To improve car performance, railroads built some refrigerator cars with extra-heavy insulation and larger bunkers (often called "super-insulated" cars). Most of these were initially 50-foot cars, allowing more capacity along with larger bunkers and heavier insulation.

Pacific Fruit Express (jointly owned by Southern Pacific and Union Pacific) experimented with the concept in 1931 by building three cars (class R-50-1) in 1931, then adding 100 cars (R-70-2) in 1932. These were 50-foot cars with a 70-ton capacity. The company would later add additional 50-foot cars for frozen foods.

The Santa Fe rebuilt 10 of its 50-foot class RR-30 cars with heavy insulation in 1936. It followed with 200 steel-sided heavy-insulation cars from General American in 1937, then another 150 in 1940 (RR-31), plus another 75 rebuilt RR-10 cars.

Western Fruit Express bought 290 heavily insulated 40-foot ice-bunker cars from Pacific Car & Foundry in 1952 and added another 550 in 1955.

Fruit Growers Express pioneered development of mechanical cars. Number 1209 was built in the FGE shops in 1956, one of 600 similar early mechanical cars on the FGE roster. The 52-foot car primarily carries frozen concentrated orange juice; it's shown in July 1961. *John Ingles, J. David Ingles collection*

Number 100028 is one of 500 class R-40-30 cars, the only series of 40-foot Pacific Fruit Express mechanical cars. Built in 1958, PFE considered it a "transition car," as it could carry either frozen food or produce. *Pacific Fruit Express*

Refrigerator car models

Plastic models are available for many refrigerator cars. Reefers have also been a popular subject of resin kits (Funaro & Camerlengo, Sunshine, Westerfield, and others). Also check Shapeways.com for 3-D printed kits of both modern and older mechanical and ice-bunker cars.

Through the steam and early diesel eras, ice-bunker frozen-food reefers would travel with produce cars in solid reefer trains or in other high-priority freights. Mechanical reefers can travel as individual cars or in blocks of cars in manifest trains.

These had sliding plug doors and otherwise looked similar to standard contemporary reefers, but carried WHIX reporting marks (HI="heavy insulation") instead of the usual WFEX marks; parent Fruit Growers Express bought identical cars, with FHIX marks.

By the early 1950s, about 2,000 super-insulated ice-bunker reefers were in service. However, frozen-food traffic was growing, and ice cars were not the ideal solution. Along with temperature-control issues, the cars required extra expense and handling time. The heavy salt use resulted in brine that drains from the cars along the track, which damaged the cars themselves and also corroded rails, bridges, and other railroad infrastructure—an issue railroads were just realizing was serious. The cars themselves suffered damage to bodies, framing, trucks, and brake gear.

The traffic that finally drove railroads toward mechanical refrigeration was the frozen juice market. The product was booming in popularity, but required even colder temperatures than other frozen foods. Although mechanical cars grew in number through the 1950s, there just weren't enough of them, and super-insulated ice cars would continue carrying some traffic through the 1950s.

Mechanical cars

Builders experimented with several methods of mechanical cooling, eventually settling on a small diesel engine to power a compressor. This equipment was housed in an enclosed compartment at one end of the car, identified by a visible screened or vented panel. The fuel tank was usually under the car.

In 1948, Fruit Growers Express, which served several railroads in the Southeast, was the first to practically test the idea, eying the growing market in frozen concentrated juice centered in Florida. After 25 cars proved their worth through 1949, FGE (which operated in partnership with Burlington Refrigerator Express and Western Fruit Express) began building additional cars, adding 175 by 1952—the year Santa Fe and PFE placed their first mechanical cars in service. By 1955, about 1,200 mechanical cars were in service.

Santa Fe's class RR-60 cars, like No. 2213, were built by the railroad's Wichita Shops in 1958. The car is 53 feet long, with smooth riveted sides, a six-foot Camel plug door, and roller-bearing trucks. *Santa Fe*

Fruit Growers Express stuck with inside-post cars for its home-built mechanical reefers. Number 11866 is a 64-foot (outside length) car with 10'-6" door built in 1963 and shown in 1969. *J. David Ingles collection*

Pacific Fruit Express shifted to external-post cars (built by Pacific Car & Foundry) in the 1960s. This is one of 400 57-foot cars in class R-70-19, built in 1968.
Pacific Fruit Express

Santa Fe built 700 cars to class RR-89 in 1966, including no. 50949. The 57-foot car has exterior-post sides and nine-foot plug doors. *J. David Ingles collection*

These early cars were exclusively for frozen-food service. Their cost (in 1955, about $21,000 compared to $13,000 for an ice-bunker car) initially precluded their economic viability for carrying produce. By 1960 about 5,000 mechanical cars had been built, and by that time most new cars had advanced, adjustable temperature controls that allowed carrying frozen foods or traditional reefer products.

Spotting features on early mechanical cars include overall length and size (most were about 50 feet, but some were 40-footers), doors (sliding plug doors of various designs, six- or eight-foot width), sides (number of panels—early cars were interior-post designs), location and style of screens/vents, roof style, end style, and side sill (straight, channel, or tabs extending down to cover the ends of the bolsters and cross bearers).

The early 1960s saw a shift to larger cars with the advent of increased weight limits. As produce traffic was declining, no new ice-bunker cars were being built, and new mechanical cars were designed to carry frozen foods as well as produce.

These new cars ranged from 55 to 65 feet (57 was a common length), and door openings became wider through the decade, to 9 and then 10 feet. Major mechanical reefer operators were PFE, FGE/BRE/WFE, and

Union Pacific rebuilt several older classes of reefers with new end-mounted refrigeration units (visible inside the opening at left), giving them ARMN reporting marks. This R-70-22 car, originally built in 1970, is shown in 2005. *Jeff Wilson*

Santa Fe; FGE and Santa Fe built large numbers of their own cars, with Pacific Car & Foundry and General American also building cars. Exterior-post cars became common in the 1960s, with the number and placement of posts (and whether any were angled) key spotting features.

Most produce traffic had left the rails for trucks by the early 1970s, as did much frozen food traffic, and operators retired all of their ice-bunker cars and many early mechanicals as their need waned. The last of this generation of mechanical cars was built in 1972; the newest cars of that period would remain the mainstay of reefer fleets through the 1990s.

Railroads by the 1990s saw an upturn in frozen food traffic, in particular frozen potato products (fries, tots, and hash browns), especially from the Pacific Northwest. These were shipped throughout the country, and the long-distance business was potentially lucrative. By the 2000s, 40 percent of frozen french fries were moving by rail (48,000 loads per year on UP alone).

This led to reconditioning many older refrigerator cars of the 1960s

In 1988, Union Pacific bought 100 new 72-foot reefers from Trinity featuring an insulated fiberglass composite body atop a heavy steel frame (class R-110-21). The bodies did not prove durable in service. *Jeff Wilson*

and '70s; notable were Union Pacific's ARMN cars, which were former PFE and FGE cars rebuilt with end-body refrigeration units (albeit still enclosed in the body end compartment). This was a temporary fix, however, as the cars were approaching the ends of their legal lifespans (40 years, or 50 with rebuilding), so they would all have to be retired by 2022.

Modern reefers

The UP in 1988 purchased new reefers from Trinity. They were an all-new design, featuring a fiberglass body atop a heavy chassis. The bodies were composite, with two layers of fiberglass sandwiching foam insulation and end-mounted refrigeration units. The 110-ton (286K GRL) cars were 7,901 cubic feet and measured 72 feet long inside

Trinity's TrinCool refrigerator cars have steel bodies and are built in 72-foot (as this BNSF car) and 64-foot inside length versions. *Jeff Wilson*

The original purpose-built Cryo-Trans carbon-dioxide refrigerated cars were built by Gunderson and were strictly for frozen foods. Number 2067 carries the logo of frozen-food maker McCain. The cars carried a warning on the doors to ventilate the car upon opening. *Jeff Wilson*

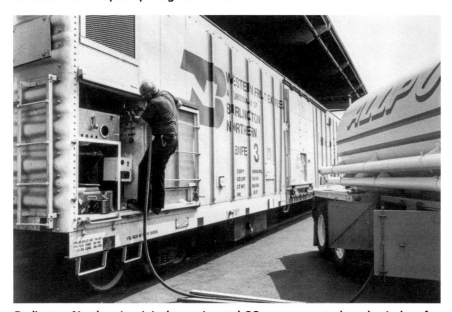

Burlington Northern's original experimental CO₂ car, converted mechanical reefer BNFE 3, receives a charge of frozen carbon dioxide from a truck in 1981. The car has been loaded with frozen french fries at Connell, Wash., and is bound for Bettendorf, Iowa. *Burlington Northern*

(83 feet outside). They were designed specifically for low-density products like frozen potatoes.

Trinity in 2000 began offering a more conventional steel-body refrigerator car, which it marketed as the TrinCool. The 110-ton car has a 7,710-cf capacity, 72-foot inside length, and 82-foot outside length, again with an end-mounted external reefer unit. This was followed by a shorter version (64-foot inside, 75-foot outside) at 6,956 cf. Both have been popular, primarily with UP and BNSF. Gunderson has also built new high-capacity refrigerator cars.

Cryogenic cars

Another solution was the cryogenic reefer, cooled by frozen carbon dioxide (CO_2). Experiments in the 1980s by Burlington Northern and others led to 45 initial cars (BN 751000-751076), all converted from older mechanical cars. Cryo-Trans added 224 rebuilt cars to its fleet from 1986-1990, mainly from old Santa Fe mechanical cars; other cars were built for J.R. Simplot (JRSX), General American (GARX), and Chrysler leasing (XTRX).

These led to the first new production cars, built by Gunderson starting in 1990. The cars had a 68-foot inside length (76 feet exterior). Once the car was sealed, it was given a 15-ton charge of CO_2, which would keep the internal temperature below zero for two weeks. These cars were strictly for frozen foods, as there was no way to regulate the temperature.

The major owner was Cryo-Trans (CRYX); other owners included

Cryo-Trans (CRYX) No. 1211 is a cryogenic refrigerator car rebuilt in 1989 from a former St. Louis Southwestern 5,482-cf boxcar. It's shown in 1986. *J. David Ingles*

Further information:

An outstanding book on refrigerator cars is *Pacific Fruit Express, Second Edition*, by Anthony W. Thompson, Robert J. Church, and Bruce H. Jones (Signature Press, 2000). Also check out *The Great Yellow Fleet*, by John H. White (Golden West Books, 1986). The book *Produce Traffic & Trains* by Jeff Wilson (Kalmbach, 2018) has information on refrigerator cars and car fleets, as well as frozen food traffic.

The original Gunderson-built cryogenic cars were all rebuilt with end refrigeration units in 2000-2001 (at the far end of this car). These cars have non-terminating corrugated ends. *Jeff Wilson collection*

GATX (Arcticars), which became involved in a patent lawsuit with Cryo-Trans; Lamb-Weston; and Simplot. Each had a distinctive paint scheme, with the CRYX cars known for their shippers' logos and city names on the cars' doors.

The CO_2 system worked well—there were no mechanical issues or refueling to worry about in transit—and was initially efficient. However, a dramatic rise in CO_2 price in the late 1990s killed the cost efficiency of the system. In 2000 and 2001, the cars were converted to standard mechanical refrigeration with the addition of end-mounted external reefer units. Cryo-Trans has since added a number of new Gunderson/Greenbrier 72-foot (inside) mechanical cars to its fleet.

CHAPTER ELEVEN

Wood chips and pulpwood

Northern Pacific 119978 is one of 300 Gunderson 100-ton wood-chip cars built for the railroad in 1967. The 60-foot car has one end door and heavy wrap-under-style side posts. It's carrying a load of chips for successor Burlington Northern in Portland, Ore., in 1993. *Jeff Wilson*

Wood pulp is the basic ingredient in making paper, including cardboard, tissue, and other products. Mills obtain pulp from both pulpwood and wood chips, both of which travel by railcar. Loadings are down compared to the late steam/early diesel era, but in 2019 railroads hauled about 40,500 loads of chips and 12,000 loads of pulpwood logs.

Bangor & Aroostook and Maine Central together bought 368 new 75-ton pulpwood cars from Magor in 1964. The 72-foot cars (64 feet between bulkheads) each held 32 cords of wood; they were the biggest pulpwood cars in service when built.
J. David Ingles

Pulpwood is the logs that become the raw material for wood pulp. They're smaller than logs used for making lumber and lumber products. Trees are sometimes grown specifically for pulp; others are those harvested that are inferior for lumber. Pulpwood is categorized by the type of wood—soft or hard—and by specific species and other qualities.

Wood chips are also a source of pulp, and come from sawmills that produce lumber or from producers that grind pulpwood on site and then ship the chips ("pulp chips"). Wood chips are also used to make lumber products such as oriented-strand board (OSB), particle board, and medium-density fiberboard (MDF).

Paper mills have historically been located near the forests that provide their raw materials. In the U.S., they are concentrated in the Pacific Northwest; New England; Upper Midwest; and in the Southeast. In Canada, they are primarily in the far east and far west regions.

Because of this, pulpwood and wood chip loads are generally short- to medium-haul traffic. Much of it historically traveled on one railroad

A Southern pulpwood car is being loaded at the Robbinsville wood yard on the Graham County (N.C.) Railroad in 1974. The car is loaded with two rows of logs.
Dan Ranger

only. Trucks were once used for short hauls; they have now taken the bulk of all pulpwood and chip traffic from railroads.

Pulpwood cars

The classic pulpwood car from the steam through early diesel eras is a bulkhead flatcar. Logs are loaded transversely on the car—often in two rows—either by hand or by a mechanical loader, most often with a claw attachment. Many pulpwood cars have decks at a shallow V angle, which cants the log stacks slightly inward, keeping them from tipping outward. Cars often had stenciling warning that logs weren't to protrude from the sides (see the Southern car on page 104).

Gondolas were often used for

The Southern rebuilt several hundred old boxcars into pulpwood flatcars in the 1950s. Number 301140 is at Manassas, Va., in 1968. Vertical lines on the bulkheads indicate the row separations. Stenciling at left reads that logs must not overhang sides by more than 10". *J. David Ingles collection*

Gondolas of (right to left) Milwaukee Road, Northern Pacific, and Great Northern carry pulpwood on Milwaukee's Chippewa Valley (Wis.) line in 1974. The line at one time served seven paper mills. *Stan Mailer*

pulpwood; typically these were 42-foot GS (general-service) cars. To increase capacity, temporary bulkheads—usually long pulp logs placed vertically along each end—were added so logs could be loaded above the car sides. Standard gons could be rotated into pulpwood service as needed, then returned to general service as traffic warranted.

Gondolas in dedicated pulpwood service were often modified. Typical changes were steel end bulkheads and vertical side extensions. To reduce car weight, floors were sometimes removed and replaced with stringers that held the logs. Sides could also have panels cut away, as well (see the Milwaukee car above). These were usually older

gondolas that would otherwise have been retired; many were listed for on-line use only.

As with other car types, pulpwood cars grew in size from 40- and 50-ton capacity in the early 1900s to 70-ton cars by the 1950s and 1960s and 100- and now 110-cars. Railroads carrying a great deal of pulpwood traffic bought new purpose-built cars for the commodity.

The advent of longer 100-ton cars in the 1960s led to logs loaded longitudinally in cars. These cars have tall side posts to contain their loads, with gaps between the posts to allow mechanical unloaders access to the logs.

Dozens of railroads carried pulpwood, and the car types varied widely among them. Check prototype photos and the *Official Railway Equipment Register* for specific information by era and railroad.

Early wood chip cars

Into the mid 1900s, wood chips from sawmills were usually considered a waste product and often burned on site. By the 1950s, lumber mills found they could profit from waste slabs and chips by selling them to paper mills, which could use them for pulp, or to mills making sheet products such as OSB.

Wood chips are extremely light, weighing about 20-25 pounds per cubic foot—less than half the density of coal. This meant that shipping chips in standard hopper cars, a common

MODELING INFO

Chip and pulpwood cars and loads

Along with plastic models, several prototype-specific kits for pulpwood and wood chip cars and loads have been offered in resin and 3-D printed plastic (such as on Shapeways.com). Look for opportunities to detail cars with pulpwood logs from real sticks (sealing them with a coat of clear flat finish is always a good idea).

An Algoma Central gondola carries a pulpwood load in 1964. The 51-foot car has wire mesh screen inside the side posts to help secure the logs.
John Ingles, J. David Ingles collection

In a scene that begs to be modeled, workers transfer pulpwood logs from trucks to gondolas by hand at a Northern Pacific team track ramp in Ironton, Minn., in January 1964. *C.F. Sager, Jeff Lemke collection*

Many modern pulpwood cars, such as Escanaba & Lake Superior 5009, have logs loaded lengthwise. Note how the wide gaps in the stakes match the rows of logs, allowing mechanical loaders to reach in and grab the logs. The white (softwood) and yellow (hardwood) marks show load limits for differing wood types. *J. David Ingles*

Louisville & Nashville was among many railroads that built wood chip cars from old hoppers. In 1962 the railroad added steel extensions to the sides of several 50-ton, two-bay, offset-side hoppers built in 1930. The rebuilds had a 3,620-cf capacity. *Louisville & Nashville*

In 1967, Pacific Great Eastern rebuilt 80 52-foot mill gondolas for chip service with extensions and end doors. The resulting cars had a 5,560-cf capacity.
J. David Ingles collection

practice into the 1950s, was inefficient. A fully loaded car by volume came nowhere near the car's 50- or 70-ton weight limit.

Profit margins on chips were small, so railroads in the 1950s built their own chip cars by modifying older hopper cars and gondolas with higher sides. These typically provided capacities of 3,500 to 4,500 cf. Railroads doing this included Boston & Maine; Canadian National; Canadian Pacific; Chesapeake & Ohio; Louisville & Nashville; Grand Trunk Western; Gulf, Mobile & Ohio; Missouri Pacific; Norfolk Southern; Pacific Great Eastern; St. Louis-San Francisco; Southern; Spokane, Portland & Seattle; and Western Maryland.

Some railroads also modified boxcars by removing the roofs and plating over the door openings, including Apache; Bangor & Aroostook; CN; CP; Maine Central; Milwaukee Road; and Southern. Other railroads have carried wood chips in bulk in standard boxcars, using paper grain doors to cover the openings, including Chicago & North Western; Dakota, Minnesota & Eastern; and Wisconsin Central.

Some railroads continued building these cars through the 1960s to alleviate the shortage of purpose-built cars that would soon be coming.

Purpose-built chip cars

As wood chip traffic increased and car capacity increased to 100-ton (263K GRL) in the early 1960s, railroads began investing in high-capacity

Wisconsin Central was among railroads that used boxcars in chip service. Disposable paper doors, reinforced by planks, contain the load; this 50-foot former Soo Line car by 1988 has had its steel doors removed and it is stenciled "WOOD CHIP LOADING ONLY." *Ted Schnepf collection*

The Apache Ry. in 1972 rebuilt built 50 old boxcars into 60-foot wood chip gondolas by splicing the bodies, plating over the door openings, and removing the roofs. The cars have a 5,800-cf capacity. *J.B. Holder, J. David Ingles collection*

purpose-built cars for wood chips. Early cars typically had capacities of 6,000-7,000 cf; some modern cars are 8,000 to 8,200 cf—double that of the home-built and converted cars of the 1950s.

Wood chip cars come in two basic types: gondola (often with one or two end doors) and hopper (bottom-dump). Railroads and mills in the northern U.S. and Canada prefer gondola-style cars. These minimize issues with moisture and freezing conditions that can cause chips to clump and plug bottom outlet doors. Customers in the southeastern U.S., where temperatures usually stay above freezing, prefer bottom-dump cars.

The first gondola-style cars were 60- to 65-foot cars built by Thrall,

Gunderson built 6,048-cf, truss-style composite-side (steel frame, plywood sheathing) wood chip cars for Great Northern, Spokane, Portland & Seattle, and Union Pacific in 1965-1966. Many, like this former GN car serving Burlington Northern in this 1994 view, were later rebuilt with steel sides. *Jeff Wilson*

FMC, and Gunderson. Specific sizes varied depending upon clearance restrictions—some were Plate C cars, but others were Plate F. They have solid sides with a top-hinged door on one or both ends. This allows them to be unloaded using either elevating end dumpers or by front-end loaders entering through the doors. They can also be unloaded by a rotary dumper.

Gondolas can be distinguished by their side styles and bracing patterns. Thrall and Gunderson both built cars with heavy vertical side posts that wrapped around under the floor, with horizontal braces between the two end panels on each side. Hooks along the tops of the side allow attaching mesh netting to keep chips from blowing out of cars in motion.

Another common style is shown by the FMC-built Montana Rail Link car below. These are larger and have shallower vertical posts with more horizontal braces among the panels. FMC also built some smooth-side (interior braced) cars for Santa Fe, Southern Pacific, and Apache.

A version built by National Steel

Railroads in the Northwest preferred gondola-style chip cars, with many mills using lifts to empty end-door cars. This is a 6,000-cf Northern Pacific car built by Thrall. *Northern Pacific*

Montana Rail Link wood chip car no. 35100 was built by FMC in 1972. The Plate F car is larger than many earlier gondola-style cars, at 6,810 cf (68'-6" interior length). It has shallow cross-pattern side braces and doors on both ends. *Jeff Wilson*

This former Southern Pacific wood chip car was built by FMC in 1975. It features smooth-side (interior-post) construction with a 7,406-cf capacity. It's rolling on successor Union Pacific rails in October 2005. *Jeff Wilson*

National Steel Car built this 6,565-cf, Plate C chip car for BC Rail in 1972. The 61'-6" (inside length) car is one of 200 in its series. *J. David Ingles collection*

Car has heavy vertical side posts only, with no horizontal members.

Gunderson in 1965-1966 built 245 composite-side cars (125 for Union Pacific, 70 for Spokane, Portland & Seattle, and 50 for Great Northern) with heavy truss-style framing and plywood walls. The plywood saved about five tons of weight compared to steel sides but deteriorated faster; most were eventually rebuilt with steel sides.

The latest chip gondolas are bathtub-style cars, with depressed floors between the trucks to increase capacity—similar to bathtub coal cars, but much larger.

Ortner built the first high-capacity bottom-dump chip car, a 7,000-cf, six-bay car for Louisville & Nashville, in 1963. Many other cars followed, built by Ortner, Magor, Greenville, and others, for CSX, Norfolk & Western, Norfolk Southern, Chesapeake & Ohio, Louisville & Nashville, and Southern.

Spotting features include the overall dimensions (and interior capacity), number of vertical posts, and number of outlet bays. The side panels vary: some have smooth panels, but many have raised panels in various patterns (rectangular with angled tapers). These give the sides additional strength, allowing thinner steel to be used compared to coal hoppers. These are all excess-height Plate F cars.

Further information

The book *Woodchip Cars* by David G. Casdorph (*Freight Cars Journal* Monograph No. 30, 1995) includes detailed spotting information for both gondola and hopper cars, with lots of roster information both by owner and manufacturer. *The Model Railroader's Guide to Industries Along the Tracks: 2* by Jeff Wilson (Kalmbach, 2006) has a chapter on the paper industry, with lots of mill and freight car images.

Eastern railroads prefer bottom-dump chip cars. Ortner built this 7,000-cf car for Louisville & Nashville in 1963. The side panels have slight vertical creases to increase strength; the steel sides are thinner on chip cars compared to coal hoppers. *Louisville & Nashville*

This Plate F, 7,526-cf, six-bay Greenville hopper-style chip car was built for Southern in 1977. Greenville's cars have embossed side panels to increase strength. *J. David Ingles*

Selected bibliography

Books

ACF Tank Cars 1980-2019 by David Casdorph. Lulu, 2020.

Box Car Production 1963-1994 by David Casdorph. Society of Freight Car Historians, 1995.

The Coil Car Directory by David Casdorph. CreateSpace Independent Publishing Platform, 2011.

Freight Cars of the '40s and '50s by Jeff Wilson. Kalmbach Books, 2015.

Mechanical Refrigerator Cars and Insulated Refrigerator Cars of the Santa Fe Railway, 1949-1988 by John B. Moore Jr. Santa Fe Railway Historical & Modeling Society, 2007.

Modern Freight Cars by Jeff Wilson. Kalmbach Media, 2019.

Pressurized Covered Hoppers by David Casdorph. Freight Cars Journal monograph no. 26, 1995.

Steam Era Freight Cars Reference Manual, Vol. 2: Tank Cars. Speedwitch Media, 2008.

Tank Cars, American Car & Foundry Company, 1865 to 1955 by Edward S. Kaminski. Signature Press, 2003.

Woodchip Cars by David Casdorph. Freight Cars Journal monograph no. 30, 1995.

Periodicals

"2,600-cubic-foot Airslide Covered Hopper Cars" by Ed Hawkins, *Railway Prototype Cyclopedia;* Part 1: No. 17 (p. 65), 2008; Part 2: No. 20 (p.86), 2010; Part 3: No. 22 (p. 75).

"6,000-Gallon Insulated High-Pressure Tank Cars from Trix Models," by Richard H. Hendrickson, *RailModel Journal,* September 2004, p. 49.

"AC&F Type 27, 10,500-Gallon, ICC-105A Propane Tank Cars," by Ed Hawkins, *Railway Prototype Cyclopedia,* Vol. 7, p. 85.

"Airslide Covered Hopper," by Bill McKean, *Mainline Modeler,* December 1986, p. 72.

"Bulk Handling of Flour Today," by W. G. Hoskins, *The Macaroni Journal,* February 1955, p. 28.

"Bulk Transportation by Trans-Flo," *Railway Age,* Nov. 4, 1950, p. 61-63.

"Coil Cars," by James Kinkaid, *Mainline Modeler,* October 1996, p. 42.

"Container Cement Gondolas of the DL&W and LV" by Gary Klein, *Flags, Diamonds & Statues,* Vol. 10, No. 3, p. 28.

"Conveying and Storing Flour Received in Bulk," by William G. Hoskins, *The Macaroni Journal,* July 1954, p. 26.

"Cryogenic Cars," by Thornton Waite, *Mainline Modeler,* August 2000, p. 26.

"GATX Arcticar," by Mark W. Heinz, *Mainline Modeler,* September 1992, p. 25.

"The History of BCR's Wood Chip Cars," by Andy Barber, *The Cariboo* (British Columbia Railway Historical & Technical Society), July 1996, p. 19.

"ICC 105 11,000-Gallon High-Pressure Tank Cars," by Richard Hendrickson, *RailModel Journal,* July 2003, p. 48.

"A Miller's Experience with Bulk Cars," by Lee Merry, *The Macaroni Journal,* July 1954, p. 21

"PFE's Mechanical Reefers," by Tony Thompson, *Railroad Model Craftsman,* January 1988, p. 76

"Santa Fe R̪-30 Class 50-Foot Refrigerator," by Richard Hendrickson, *RailModel Journal,* September 2006, p. 18.

"Walthers HO & N Scale 76-Foot Cryogenic Reefers," by Scott Chatfield, *RailModel Journal,* March 1994, p. 5.

Miscellaneous

Association of American Railroads, various data sheets, rail traffic data, and *Manual of Standards and Recommended Practices* (aar.com).

Car Builders' Cyclopedia. Various editions. Simmons-Boardman.

"Cement: Mineral Commodity Profiles," report by William B. Hall and Robert E. Ela., Bureau of Mines, U.S. Department of the Interior, November 1978.

Ensuring Railroad Tank Car Safety. Transportation Research Board, National Research Council, National Academy of Sciences, 1994.

The Freight Traffic Red Book. Various editions.

GATX Airslide operating manual. General American.

The Official Railway Equipment Register. Various editions

Railroad Car Facts: Statistics on Car Building and Car Repairing. Various issues. American Railway Car Institute.

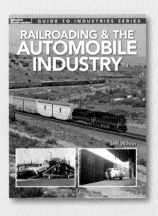
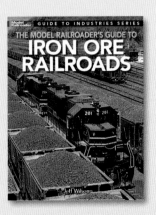
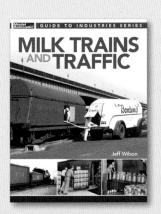